US OPEN
UNMATCHED

US OPEN

UNMATCHED

A CELEBRATION OF AMERICA'S PREMIER TENNIS EXPERIENCE

Edited by
Mark Preston and Rick Rennert

UNITED STATES TENNIS ASSOCIATION

UNIVERSE

Acknowledgments

The editors owe a debt of gratitude to Arlen Kantarian, who made this project possible and who, along with David Newman, provided us with valuable advice and encouragement throughout this project.

We give special thanks to the current USTA leadership, most notably Merv Heller and Rick Ferman, for their constant support.

We would also like to thank our designer, Kirsten Navin, who has worked with infinite patience, sensitivity, and skill to bring this book together.

Design: **Kirsten Navin**

UNITED STATES TENNIS ASSOCIATION
70 West Red Oak Lane • White Plains, NY
10604-3502 • USTA.com

First published in the United States of America in 2002
by **UNIVERSE PUBLISHING**
A Division of Rizzoli International Publications, Inc.
300 Park Avenue South
New York, NY 10010

2002 2003 2004 2005 2006 / 10 9 8 7 6 5 4 3 2 1

Printed in the United States

Preceding pages:

Andre Agassi wins his first US Open title, 1994.

Arthur Ashe

Billie Jean King

John McEnroe

Chris Evert and Jimmy Connors outside Forest Hills' West Side Tennis Club, 1972.

Pete Sampras

Serena and Venus Williams

Andy Roddick

CONTENTS

The Newport Casino

Introduction

BY BUD COLLINS

WHERE WERE FREDERICK ELDRIDGE and Berkeley Mostyn?

Did they oversleep? Could they have been bageled by hangovers? We will never know why Eldridge and Mostyn were the no-shows among 26 pioneering guys entered—though not quite sure what they were up to—in the original tennis championship of the United States in 1881. Who's to say that, if they had appeared, either Eldridge or Mostyn would not have been first in a long line of champions winding through three centuries from Newport (R.I.) to New York. Instead, that honor was seized on the lawn of the Newport Casino by a 19-year-old Harvard student from Boston, Dick Sears.

THE OCCASION, AT THE CLOSE OF THE summer of 1881, was a far cry (and some 200 miles) from Flushing Meadows. After all, this game was merely seven years old, and four years beyond the first Wimbledon, granddaddy of all tournaments.

Arthur Ashe & Stan Smith

Newport witnesses, a handful of the mildly curious seated on folding chairs or standing, did, however, make it a profitable event: $4.32 net after expenses were subtracted from gate receipts.

But it really was light years removed from the glare of floodlights on an asphalt-floored sporting canyon called Arthur Ashe Stadium that now stands as the centerpiece of the USTA National Tennis Center. From there, the red eyes of TV cameras transport that late-summer scene of sport and spectacle across the planet to millions of gawkers who can't be among the assemblage of 23,000 cheering, say, a household battle between sisters named Venus and Serena for the championship of their country. That, and an incidental reward of hundreds of thousands of dollars. Profits, like viewers, are now measured in the millions.

Oh, there had been sisters previously involved at the climactic stages—110 years previously. Ellen Roosevelt, defending her championship of 1890, lost it in the title match to Mabel Cahill of Ireland, a round after sister Grace was also beaten by Cahill, the spoiler of a Roosevelt monopoly. Yet, who knew? At least beyond a small circle. Well, perhaps a future U.S. president, nine-year-old Franklin Roosevelt of Hyde Park, N.Y., was aware of his neighboring cousins' prowess with racquets.

![John McEnroe]

John McEnroe

Still, as lightly regarded as tennis was, such early stalwarts as the Roosevelts and Cahill were trailblazers in a brilliant parade over the decades as the United States Championships (evolving as the US Open in 1968) developed into an internationally celebrated colossus. An ever-revitalized pageant, blending superb and inspirational athleticism, exhilarating combat, laughter and tears, tension and relief, fun and dismay, it offers us myriad dramas played out on rectangular stages.

THE GAME—AND THE TOURNAMENT— turned upside-down in 1968, a year of radical change and upheaval throughout the world. After years of agitation to bring together the best players, amateur and professional, emulating the longtime custom of golf—suddenly "open tennis" happened! Prodded by Wimbledon, and progressive USTA President Robert Kelleher, the International Tennis

Jimmy Connors

Federation's defenders of status quo and what had become phony amateurism were overrun.

Abruptly, trophies were accompanied by prize money (a then-dazzling pot of $100,000 at the freshly minted US Open), but none of it went to the stupefying, odds-defying champion from Virginia, Arthur Ashe. A 25-year-old lieutenant in the U.S. Army, he was required to remain amateur to maintain Davis Cup eligibility, conforming to regulations of the time. Arthur's victim in a gripping five-set final, pro Tom Okker, got the $14,000 first prize, while the champ reaped exactly $28.00 in per diem expenses.

Hopeful, but wary of the new, professionalized scheme, the USTA conceived a U.S. Amateur Championship as well to continue tradition, a fall-back if "Opens" didn't click. It was held at Longwood in Boston a week prior to the US Open, the trophies won by Ashe and Aussie Margaret Court.

Regardless of Ashe's impressive five-set victory over Bob Lutz (the first time he'd been seen nationally on TV, via PBS), he was lightly regarded, fifth seeded, among the reunion of high-powered pros at Forest Hills.

Nine former champions surrounded Ashe, eight of them pros. One, 52-year-old Frank Parker, the 1944-45 ruler, just wanted to be in on the cataclysmic alterations. Nevertheless, the admirable, go-for-broke strokesman Ashe, an obvious representative of change—the first man of color to win—zoomed

Chris Evert & Martina Navratilova

through a charmed fortnight to complete an unsurpassable feat: U.S. Amateur and Open championships in the same year. The U.S. Amateur tourney continues, but no one will repeat that extravagant double.

Since no female pro tour had existed, the women carried on with the usual cast. England's Virginia Wade, an amateur while winning the initial open event, the British Hard Court Championships, five months before, upset defending champ Billie Jean King for the title, and opted to take the money, a whopping $6,000.

But the effervescent Californian Billie Jean, forceful crusader and volleyer—"Mother Freedom" of the women's cause—won again in 1971-72 and 1974. But she will be best-remembered for preaching equality of the sexes (as well as that Astrodome schlockodrama, her 1973 put-down of 1939 champ Bobby Riggs). By that time the USTA had come around to B.J.'s revolutionary way of thinking, offering identical prize money to women and men.

In 1969, it took F. D. Robbins 100 games (22-20, 9-7, 6-8, 8-10, 6-4) to subdue Dick Dell in the first round, a wearying record. Goodbye to that deucedly sort of thing was waved in 1970 by the adoption of Jimmy Van Alen's brainchild, the tie-breaker. The U.S. led the way in the innovation's installation, and lanky

Stan Smith was the first to conclude a men's championship in a breaker, over Czech Jan Kodes in 1971.

Also revolutionizing the game were two kids, amateurs and future all-timers, who showed up in the early '70s: Floridian Chris Evert, 16, and Illinois lefty Jimmy Connors, 17. They (along with the Swede, Bjorn Borg) did it with two-fisted backhands, strange-looking then.

In 1971, Evert ignited the "Chrissie Craze," cutting a swath to the semis. Captivating hearts and capturing victories through 1989, Evert amassed six titles and 101 singles match wins, many more than anyone else but Connors's 98.

Ivan Lendl

Jimmy, the "Brash Basher of Belleville," went out fast in 1970. But his fire never did, heating adoring congregations at Flushing right through the amazing dash to the 1991 semis, and his 40th birthday party, a first-round win a year later. Beginning a five-title collection in 1974 on the grass blades, he continued in 1976, beating Borg on clay. A hard man on the Center's hard courts in 1978, 1982-83, Connors is an historic loner in ruling the U.S. on all three surfaces.

Jimmy's final-round problems were posed in left-handed Spanish by Spaniard Manolo Orantes in 1975 and Argentine Guillermo Vilas in 1977, dirt-kickers who rejoiced in the U.S.'s quickly passing fancy for clay. Vilas's triumph, inducing ecstatic Latin supporters to dance onto the court, bade farewell to the ivy-clad Forest Hills Stadium and its sentinels, the concrete eagles on the rim.

Youth was the theme in 1979 as the victors totaled 36 years, the youngest of all championship combinations: Tracy Austin, 16, and left-handed John McEnroe, 20. She, two months younger than 1951 champ Maureen Connolly, seemed a guest at the Teddy Bears Picnic, barely 100 pounds in a homemade pinafore. But Tracy, another of the

Steffi Graf

California queens, was steely with a double-barrelled backhand from the backcourt in dethroning Evert. She won again two years later over the acrobatic volleying of marvelous Martina Navratilova. But Martina's championship times would come—only after surviving a frustrating, fruitless decade—in 1983-84 and 1986-87. The first two victimized Evert, with whom she waged and won a ferocious-yet-friendly feud of 80 matches (43-37) over 16 years.

Despite his eminence, the iron-willed Swede could never solve the US Open: zero for 10 visits. "Mac the Knife," the first since Tilden in 1922 to win three straight, added 1984. Not since Malcolm Whitman in 1900 had a New Yorker reigned; now McEnroe owned this New York spectacular.

P e t e   S a m p r a s

Martina, who won four US Open doubles titles with Pam Shriver (and a 1987 triple), had a 3-1 edge over Evert at the Open.

Distinguished by a velvet touch and steel wool temperament, McEnroe enraptured and enraged as the competitive flame burned through 1992 and four titles, notably the enthralling 1980 and 1981 battles with Borg.

Ah, but yet another three-straighter was in the wings: stolid, solid, determined Ivan Lendl from Czechoslovakia. Pushing McEnroe off the throne, ramrod-built Ivan won again in 1986 and 1987. Though he lost the titles of 1982-83 to Connors, of 1988 to unerring Swede Mats Wilander, and of 1989 to the net-charging German Boris Becker, he equaled Tilden's record of eight consecutive final appearances.

By ambushing Wilander in the second round of 1989, a quiet, loosely gaited California teenager named Pete Sampras served punishingly while serving notice that he'd

Patrick Rafter

be a factor for a long time. So did another teen phenom, a flamboyant one from Las Vegas named Andre Agassi, who made the semifinals. Twelve months later, they would be ready to forge a torrid rivalry that has glittered at the uppermost level to this day. The final of 1990 was Pete's day, the victory over Andre setting him apart, barely 19, as the greenest of all U.S. male champions, undercutting by four months another 19-year-old of a

Lindsay Davenport

Serena Williams

century earlier, Oliver Campbell.

These two greats-to-be were perfect foils: Pete, the smooth, marauding volleyer; Andre, the slick, accurate counterpuncher. They were ringleaders of the finest crop of American men, also embracing finalists Jim Courier of 1991, Michael Chang of 1996, Todd Martin of 1999, and MaliVai Washington, Wimbledon finalist of 1996.

Within Pete's record bag of major singles championships are three other US Opens: 1993 and 1995-96. The last is best recalled primarily for his gamely squelching a fifth-set match point in the agonizing quarterfinal victory over Alex Corretja while ill, reeling and vomiting.

Andre, rebounding from a slump, won in 1994 even though ranked No. 20, the only unseeded victor of the Open era, and the first in 24 years, since Australia's Fred Stolle. He was back up there, seeded No. 2, while taking his second Open title in 1999.

Following her Grand Slam, Steffi Graf, a German zephyr with blonde tresses flying (today Mrs. Andre Agassi), piled up four more titles in 1989, 1993, and 1995-96. She was given pause by Gabriela Sabatini in the 1990 final and gave way to others as Monica Seles came along as the unorthodox empress of 1991-92. Monica is unique with her shriek accompanied by growling groundies struck by both hands on both sides. The "Barcelona Bumblebee," Arantxa Sanchez-Vicario, flitted past Graf to win in 1994.

As the farthest outsider to grace a final, regal at 6-feet-2 with beaded coiffure, teenager Venus Williams was ranked No. 66 in her Open debut. No unseeded starter had done so spectacularly other than Darlene Hard, beaten by Althea Gibson in 1958. Swift and brimming over with firepower, Venus lost the clash of 17-year-olds to Swiss Martina Hingis. But, like Hard (1960-61), she was a champion-to-be, 2000 and 2001, succeeding, of all people, another concussive Williams, little sister Serena. Serena at 17 had deposed 1998 champ Lindsay Davenport.

One family, three consecutive titles. Nothing like that keeping-it-in-the-family act had ever happened anywhere.

Australia was heard from again, a quarter-century drought ended by a man from the parched Outback,

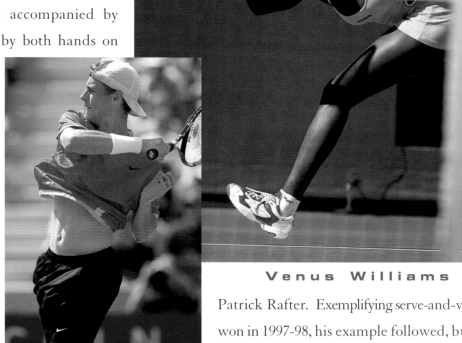

Venus Williams

Lleyton Hewitt

Patrick Rafter. Exemplifying serve-and-volley, he won in 1997-98, his example followed, but from the baseline, by the youngest of the Aussie tribe's U.S. champs, 20-year-old Lleyton Hewitt in 2001. Hewitt put a final-round dent in Sampras, as did another 20-year-old, that boyish bear of a Russian in 2000, Marat Safin.

The most physically imposing of all their majesties at 6-foot-4 and 200 pounds, the first of his country to reign, muscular Muscovite Safin would have been quite a sight at that inaugural conclave at Newport in 1881. That's where it all began, without those truants Frederick Eldridge and Berkeley Mostyn.

Poor fellows—they missed all the fun.

USTA NATI

1ˢᵗ SET

Setting the
Stage

When the US Open left behind the serene surroundings of Forest Hills in 1978 for the urban sprawl of Flushing Meadows, a new era of tennis began. The Open no longer belonged to the country club, it now belonged to the country.

Upon these acres of cement have grown the game's grandest stages, floorboards for an annual display of one of the world's greatest sports and entertainment extravaganzas, featuring the world's toughest tennis.

Indeed, these grounds, which once hosted the World's Fair, now each year host the world, fans from all corners of the globe flocking to the USTA National Tennis Center as the USTA presents this grand happening known as the US Open. For one late-summer fortnight, New York, and, more specifically, this great, hard-floored expanse, is the center of the sporting world, its players and audience generating a palpable energy that surges from this place, sending forth a singular crackle of high-voltage electricity.

Crowning achievement:
The USTA National Tennis Center in Flushing Meadows provides a stage upon which performers may sculpt greatness.

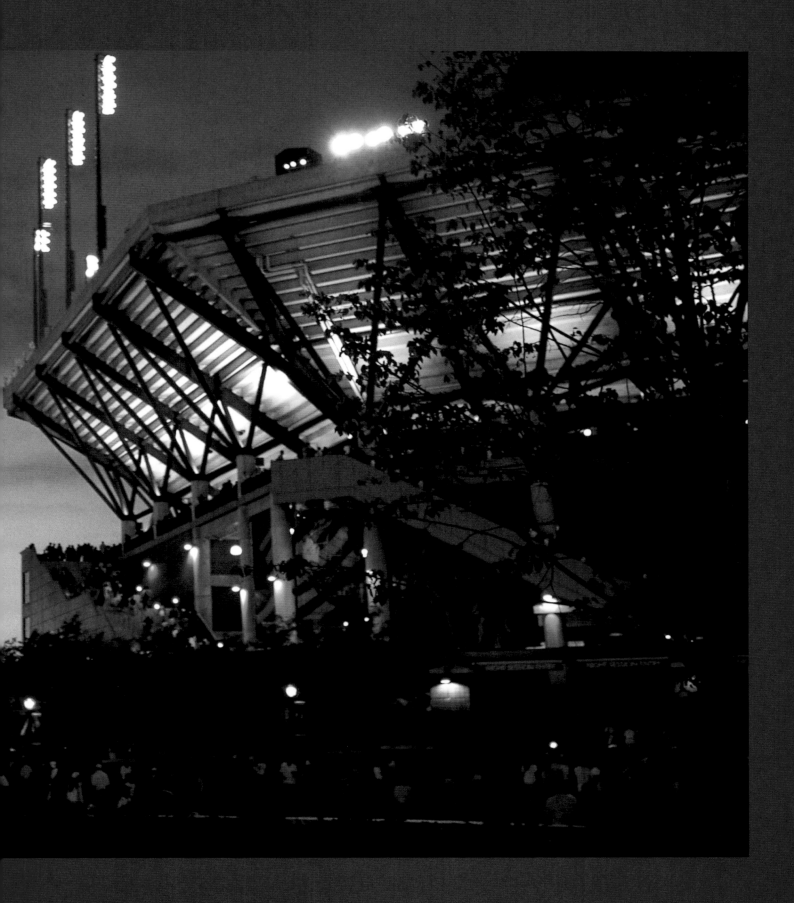

Hot seats:
US Open tickets have long been
a sizzling commodity.

A clean winner:
The NTC staff help the Open shine (left).

Supporting cast:
Once the first ball is struck, these ballboys (below) will shadow every second of play.

Practice makes perfect:
Andre Agassi (above) and Anna Kournikova (middle, right) fine-tune their games before the feature performance.

Following directions:
The daily drawsheet provides fans (above, right) with a map to the most entertaining stops.

Based on balls:
Keeping these little yellow spheres in play can be a handful.

Super-structure:
Arthur Ashe Stadium (right) is widely recognized as the game's grandest stage.

Standard bearers:
The festive past champions banners (opposite) herald those who've made their mark at Flushing Meadows.

Global appeal:
The unisphere from the 1964-65 World's Fair (right) still welcomes the world to an unforgettable festival.

View to a thrill:
Overflow crowds (below) create seats ouside the stands.

Arthur
ASHE

BY JOHN FEINSTEIN

I T MAY WELL BE THAT ONLY HISTORY WILL BE able to truly measure Arthur Ashe. Certainly mere numbers can't do it. Ashe had a distinguished career that included victories in the US and Australian Opens and at Wimbledon. He was a Davis Cup star and a Davis Cup captain. He was a doubles finalist at all four majors with four different partners, and he might very well have added to all that if health problems hadn't slowed him in the latter stages of his career.

But Ashe's place in the history of the game—and in the history of the US Open—goes well beyond places any numbers may take you. He grew up in the segregated South at a time when the words "black" and "tennis player" rarely appeared next to one another. He dealt with all the pain that came with being an almost solitary black figure in a white world and never complained about it, never used it as an excuse—however legitimate—for any of his failures. He simply continued to grow as a player and a person.

He was not only the first black man to win a U.S. Championship, he remains the only black man to have done so. In fact, Ashe won two U.S. titles in the same year, first winning the U.S. Championships—played at Longwood outside of Boston in that strange year of 1968, when tennis was in the process of becoming "open" to professionals. Two weeks later, he captured the inaugural US Open at Forest Hills.

Ashe beat Tom Okker in a dramatic five-set final to win the Open on a Monday afternoon in a half-empty stadium. Okker pocketed the $14,000 first prize because Ashe was an amateur, an Army lieutenant stationed at West Point. Vietnam was very much a part of American life at that time, and Ashe wore his Army uniform in and out of the stadium on the day of his victory.

Winning that first Open—which was also the first championship on live network TV—made Ashe into a celebrity, a role he was never comfortable with. But, as with so many other challenges in his life, Ashe rose to the occasion. He became more outspoken politically and, after heart problems forced him to retire as a player at 34, he became a quiet force on many important issues. He was the rarest of athletes: someone who made a larger impact on society after his playing career than during his playing career. As brilliant as Arthur Ashe the tennis player was, he was only a small part of what Arthur Ashe the man went on to become.

Even in his final days, Ashe understood that much of the work he had started needed to continue. Though he and John McEnroe had more than their share of battles when Ashe was captaining McEnroe on Davis Cup teams, Ashe always saw McEnroe as the one who could carry the standard when he was gone. Because of his respect for Ashe, McEnroe has worked hard to see that programs started by Ashe have continued. On the night Arthur Ashe Stadium was dedicated, the Master of Ceremonies was McEnroe.

Ashe played a lot of brilliant tennis. But the mark that he made on the sport—and on the world—goes well beyond the borders of any court or stadium. He wouldn't have wanted it to be any other way.

Arthur Ashe Kids' Day

THE US OPEN GETS ROLLING EACH year with Arthur Ashe Kids' Day, a tennis and music festival featuring star-studded entertainment and lots of kids' activities—including tennis clinics and interactive games. The event honors tennis legend and humanitarian Arthur Ashe and benefits the USA Tennis National Junior Tennis League—a program that Ashe co-founded and brings tennis to economically disadvantaged children. Headliners over the years include Hanson, the Backstreet Boys, Britney Spears, 98°, Jessica Simpson, O-Town, and Lil' Bow Wow, as well as Bill Cosby, Rosie O'Donnell, and Jennifer Love Hewitt.

WELCOME TO
ARTHUR ASHE
KIDS' DAY
A USTA Event
Presented by ALTNA

Billie Jean
KING

BY STEVE FLINK

T HERE SHE WAS, THOROUGHLY IN HER element, taking on Evonne Goolagong in the 1974 US Open final on the capricious grass at Forest Hills. Only a year earlier, the redoubtable Billie Jean King had overcome Bobby Riggs at the highly charged "Battle of the Sexes" in Houston. By responding with such gumption to the challenge of Riggs, King sparked intrigue in tennis among sports fans who previously would have paid no attention to her sport.

King and Goolagong performed with astonishing vigor and panache. As King recently recalled, "The crowd was wonderful. The stadium was absolutely chock full, so packed that people were sitting down on the grass at courtside. It was the first time I had seen so much electricity in the air. I thought it was a huge step forward for tennis. Since I had played Bobby, men's and women's attendance at tournaments had gone off the charts. It was a great time for the game."

All through that exhilarating afternoon, King was stretched to her physical and emotional limits by her Australian rival. Goolagong's sparkling, free-wheeling, exuberant play delighted the audience. King had no alternative but to produce her best brand of attacking percentage tennis. Billie Jean rescued herself from 0-3 in the final set to prevail 3-6, 6-3, 7-5. Both players were so inspired that they left the fans gasping in admiration. It was the fourth and last time that King would capture the championship of her country, and one of the crowning moments of her career.

"Evonne was so creative," says Billie Jean. "It was one of my favorite singles matches, a great match made even more terrific because I have never seen a court in such bad shape for a final. Evonne was always ahead of me but somehow I ended up winning. I felt like a guardian angel took care of me."

Billie Jean was so exhausted and debilitated after a long summer of World TeamTennis that she had strongly considered skipping that Open. "At the last second," she remembers, "I decided to enter even though I was totally tapped. But I thought I would lose in the first or second round."

King clearly felt fortunate to win that tournament. But the cognoscenti believed that this was Billie Jean close to the peak of her powers, and recognized that Billie Jean at 30 was a ferocious competitor who made her own breaks. It was no accident that she came through when it counted in a city she adopted as her own. She says, "New York has been my primary or secondary residence since 1975. I feel like I am part of the fabric of the community."

Billie Jean might well have won more US Opens had she not been so absorbed by critical political developments both before and after Open tennis started in 1968. The fact remains that in her prime, from 1971-74, King was victorious three out of four years. As she concludes, "I helped change the game to make it more inclusive, to make it an honest sport. I could finally breathe by the time I won the Open for the final time. The women had one voice because of the WTA, which I founded. Winning the Open in '74 was the culmination of a lot of things for me. I really felt at peace because I believed I had made a positive difference for tennis."

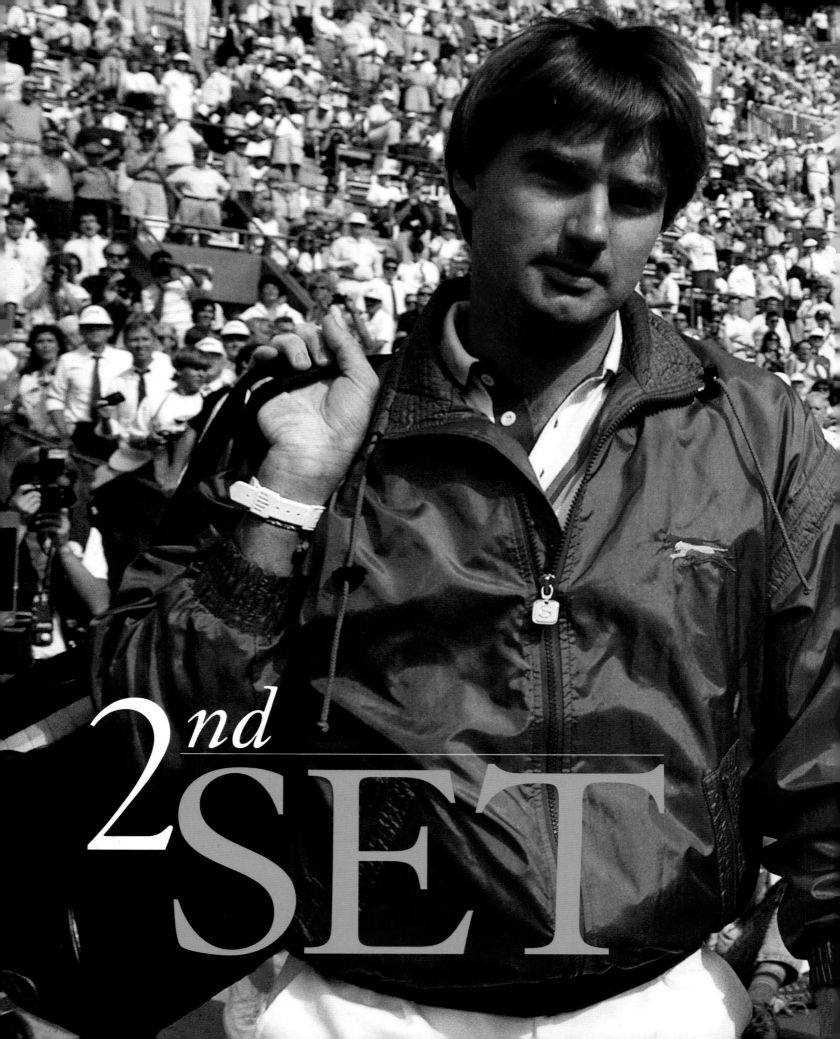

2nd SET

Ready, Play

The words made famous by Francis Albert Sinatra are inscribed above the tunnel leading the players from the labyrinth of the stadium underbelly onto the great stage of Arthur Ashe Stadium court: "If I can make it there, I'll make it anywhere." Indeed, this is the place where legends are born and return to prove that they still merit that moniker.

Each effort at proving you belong begins with a solitary walk, an introspective stroll that may or may not lead to eventual greatness. Through the tunnels, into the light, out alone before 23,000 who expect—demand—that you will leave everything you have right here on this floor before them. You'll do so, knowing all the while that they demand the same from that person on the other side of the net. All of your thoughts, all of your energy channel inward in those moments before the match begins. With the first serve, all of it explodes outward. In a matter of time, the numbers on the scoreboard will let you know if you've brought enough.

A march toward greatness:
Legends line the walls and walk the halls of the tunnel into Ashe Stadium (left).
Picture perfect:
Chris Evert and Tracy Austin (above) were the leading ladies of several Open casting calls.

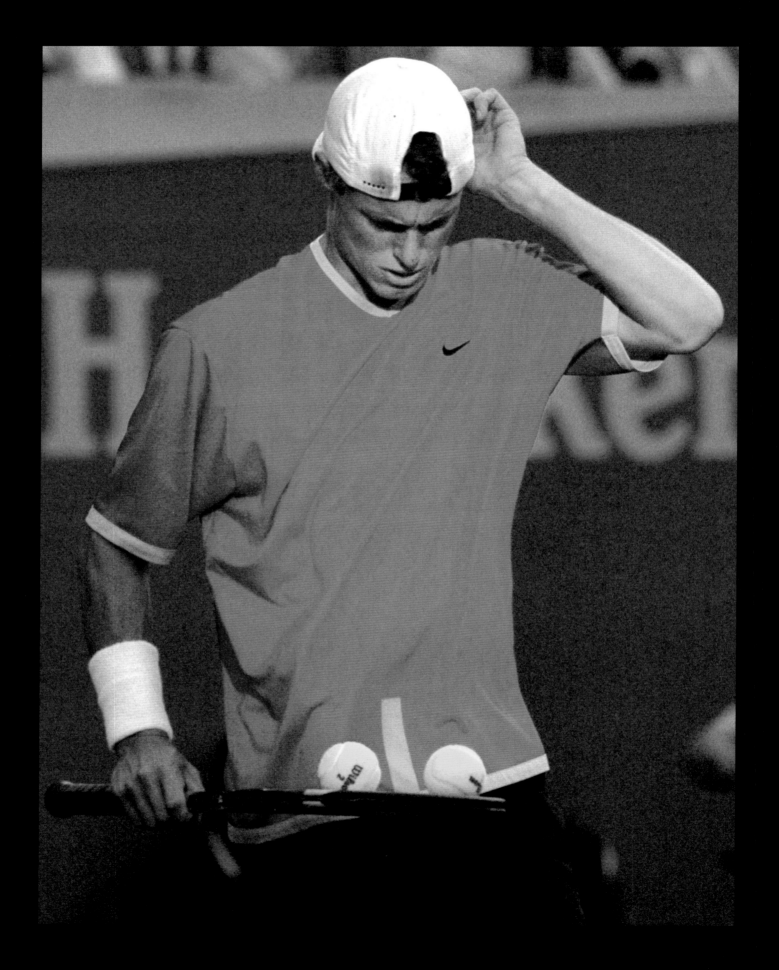

Into the light:
Lleyton Hewitt (opposite) shone brilliantly in winning the 2001 title.

Tale of the tape:
Bjorn Borg (upper left) and Vitas Gerulaitis (above) prep for play.

Net results:
A let-cord judge (left) specializes in touch shots.

Two for the show:
Like a painted warrior, John McEnroe (above) chooses his weapon
before doing battle.

Made in the shade:
Jennifer Capriati (opposite) goes undercover to collect her thoughts.

Jimmy
CONNORS

BY JOHN FEINSTEIN

THE BEST WAY TO DESCRIBE THE RELATIONSHIP between James Scott Connors and the United States Open is simple: he loved it and it loved him.

It wasn't just the five victories on three different surfaces (grass, 1974; clay, 1976; hardcourt, 1978, 1982, and 1983), it was the whole Connors thing—the way he fed on the crowd's emotions, the way the crowd fed on *his* emotions. He reached his first Open semifinal in 1974 and his last one in 1991. He was a darling in '74 because he was engaged to Chris Evert and his bad-boy image was cool. He was a darling in '91 because he was 39 and the sage father of two adorable kids. In between, he played some of the most dramatic, entertaining, and emotional tennis ever seen.

Connors often described his relationship with the New York crowd by talking about the fact that it loved to see "blood and guts all over the court. They know I'll give them that every time out, whether I win or lose, I'll spill my guts out there before I'm done."

What would happen, he was asked, if he spilled his guts in similar fashion at Wimbledon? Connors smiled his famous bad-boy smile and said, "They'd ask me to clean 'em up."

No one ever asked Connors to clean anything up at the Open. John McEnroe won four times after the tournament moved to the USTA National Tennis Center in 1978 (he and Connors won the first seven men's championships contested there), but there was never any doubt that Louis Armstrong Stadium was Connors's stage. He owned the place, especially at night, especially in the fifth set of a tight match because the

crowd knew—just knew—that Connors was going to find a way to win. More often than not, he did.

What made Connors such a beloved hero wasn't just the wins or the losses but his endurance. Consider this: he played his first Open final against Ken Rosewall, who was born in 1934. He played his last Open semifinal against Jim Courier, who was born in 1970. Tennis fans, particularly those at the Open, where he played 115 matches over a span of 22 years, watched him grow up. He first showed up in 1970 as the about-to-be-18-year-old Belleville Belter. He wasn't done until 1992, when he exited as the game's grand old man at 40.

By then, he had written and re-written record books and given every tennis fan a Jimmy Connors story to tell. His extraordinary run to the semi-finals in 1991 at the age of 30 may have been his finest hour—an hour that played out for two weeks. He had been injured and missed the Open in 1990. But he came flailing back in '91, pulling off one magical comeback after another—Patrick McEnroe and Aaron Krickstein to this day can't figure out how they lost those matches—before finally being stopped by an ascendant 21-year-old Courier.

In a sense, the loss didn't matter. Connors had already won by being there. Tennis had won, too. Connors was on the front page of *The New York Times* and Ted Koppel convened panels to discuss the magical mystery tour of Jimmy Connors. He was that good, that remarkable.

The New York crowd—the Open crowd—loved every second of it. So did Connors, every last blood and guts moment.

Kuerten call:
Gustavo Kuerten (above) angles for a winner.

Toss-up:
Lindsay Davenport (opposite) prepares to make her point.

Swede dreams:
The ever-cool Stefan Edberg (opposite) delivers a scorching salvo.

Armed and dangerous:
Anna Kournikova (right) extends herself on the serve.

Express Courier:
Jim Courier (below) mastered the rapid delivery.

Framed:
Martina Hingis (below, right) is a profile in perfection.

They also serve:
Ballkids (above) await the call to retrieve those serves that miss
their mark.

Special delivery:
Patrick Rafter, Serena Williams, Jennifer Capriati, and Andre Agassi
(opposite, clockwise from top left) prove a formidable foursome.

Chris EVERT

BY STEVE FLINK

IF THERE WAS ONE MAJOR TOURNAMENT that put Chris Evert on the map and kept her there, it was surely the US Open. The immensely popular Floridian made a spectacular debut in the summer of 1971, surging to the semifinals as a 16-year-old. She came into that Open as an enormously promising player who had created extraordinary curiosity about herself, and came away as a celebrity.

In that astonishing fortnight at Forest Hills, she was seen on national television for the first time in a career-defining match against countrywoman Mary Ann Eisel, saving six match points to seal the victory. Thereafter, she knocked out veterans Francoise Durr and Lesley Hunt. It took a resolute Billie Jean King to stop the implacable Evert.

As Chris reflects more than three decades later, "I went from being pretty much a top junior who had not been exposed much to professional tennis to reaching the semifinals. It was like a fairy tale." She had made her mark irrevocably with admirable

poise under pressure, and her trademark two-handed back-hand. Moreover, Evert also won the permanent affection of the fans. As Chris says, "I grew up over the years right in front of the public's eyes. It was a very patriotic era when I played. I came after Billie Jean and then Jimmy Connors and John McEnroe came along. It wasn't so much me as an individual as it was a package deal of being part of a great American era when there were so many diehard fans."

Evert appeared in 19 consecutive Opens, reaching at least the quarterfinals every year from 1971-89, winning six championships in the process. After four straight semifinal losses on the grass at Forest Hills, she broke the barrier on Har-Tru in 1975, moving past Evonne Goolagong in a tense three-set final. That was her first of four championships in a row, and then her crown was taken away in the 1979 final by 16-year-old Tracy Austin. Austin had ousted Evert five times in a row at various tournaments as they approached a US Open semifinal confrontation in 1980. Rarely had Chris needed a triumph more. She cast Austin aside 4-6, 6-1, 6-1 with supreme tactical acuity. Evert called her father in Fort Lauderdale and told him that she won, then burst into tears before asking him to fly up to watch her in the final. Jimmy Evert—proud father and coach—was in the stands the next day to watch his daughter win a major in person for the first time.

Four years later, she took the first set from Martina Navratilova in the final, only to lose in three sets. Evert told friends through her tears, "I wish I could have won this match. It would have been the perfect way for me to retire."

As it was, her last tournament was the 1989 US Open. There, she routed Monica Seles 6-0, 6-2 in one of her most inspired matches ever. That set up a quarterfinal appointment with Zina Garrison, when Chris was uneven and out of sorts, bowing 7-6, 6-2. As Evert reflects, "I just didn't have the competitive fires. I had gone through the whole circle of life at the US Open. That is where it had all started for me, and where it ended."

Twisted mister:
Carlos Moya (above) manages to keep his head in the game.

Going on-line:
An official (above, right) earns his stripes.

Swede and sour:
Mats Wilander (right) begs to differ.

Head-to-head:
Monica Seles (above) is always a picture of focus.

Shadow boxing:
Forms of perfection (left) are carved out on these courts.

61

Forward motion:
Andy Roddick's rocket serve (left) has lifted him into the game's upper echelon.

Ruffles and flourishes:
Jana Novotna's easy style (above) makes serving seem a breeze.

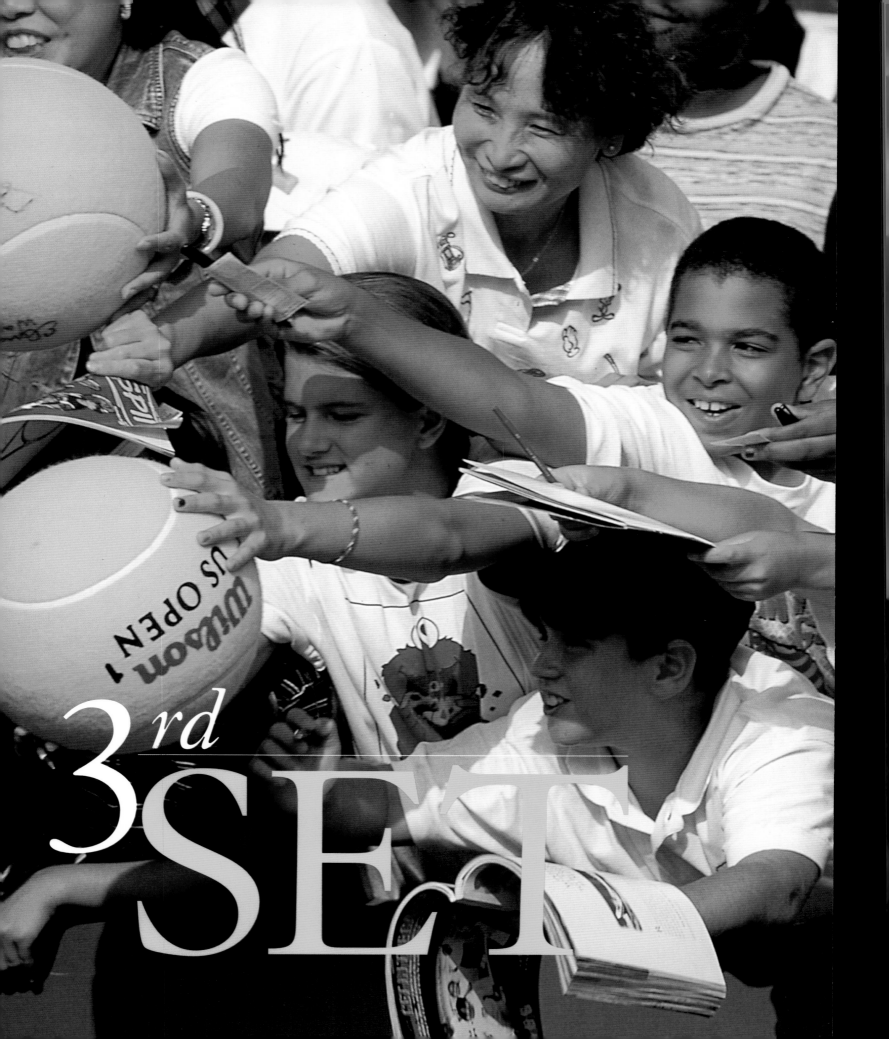

3rd SET

Outside the
Lines

It is equal parts sport and spectacle, this US Open. World-class athletes performing for world-wise fans. Add world-class entertainment to that mix and you've got a bona fide happening—an extravaganza that you've just got to see, an unforgettable party at which you've just got to be seen.

The Open is New York; it reflects the Big Apple to its core: frenetic, fast-paced, more than a little bit crazy. Maybe it's the heat from the late-summer sun; maybe it's the heat that sparks from the hard-court friction. Whatever lights the fire, it sizzles—uncontrolled—for 14 days.

At no other sporting event are the fans such a tangible part of the event itself, collectively a living, breathing entity that infuses life into the event on a daily—and nightly—basis. Famous faces and those less famous share a commonality here. They all want to be close to the fire.

Pen pal:
Jennifer Capriati (left) signs in for her fans.

Spreading cheer:
US Open action (above) brings fans to their feet.

License to thrill:
The Open is deep in the heart of this Texas fan (top, left).

A monumental event:
Lady Liberty (top, right) carries a torch for the world's toughest tennis.

Pinned down:
A young collector (above) and his major in-vest-ment.

An unmistakable buzz:
Some fans (right) allow the Open to go to their heads.

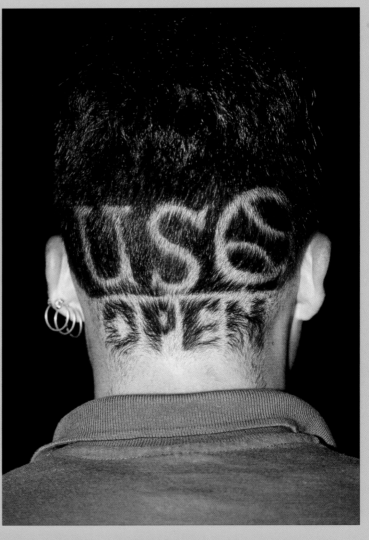

Tuning in:
A crowd gathers in the plaza in front of Arthur Ashe Stadium (top) to enjoy some off-court harmony.

All that jazz:
A hot band (above) provides cool entertainment.

A tall tale:
Some US Open sights (above) truly must be seen to be

John
MCENROE

BY JOHN FEINSTEIN

W HEN SOMEONE WINS FOUR UNITED STATES Opens, there are bound to be many memorable moments in that career. But if there is a quintessential John McEnroe US Open moment, it came in 1980, during the final against Bjorn Borg, his great rival and friend.

This was two months after McEnroe and Borg had staged their classic Wimbledon final, the one in which McEnroe won an 18-16 fourth-set tie-break before Borg hung on to win the fifth set—and his fifth straight Wimbledon title. That victory gave Borg the first two legs of the Grand Slam (the Australian Open was then played at the end of the year), and he arrived in New York looking for his first U.S. championship, the third step en route to that Grand Slam.

Only McEnroe, it seemed, stood between Borg and a feat accomplished by only two other men before him. McEnroe knew that. He had won his first Open a year earlier, beating fellow New Yorker Vitas Gerulaitis in the final. This, though, was different. This was Borg on McEnroe's turf, playing him in a stadium only a few miles from where he had grown up.

McEnroe won the first two sets. Then Borg, indomitable as ever, won the next two. The sun was down by now, the stadium so loud it was almost impossible to hear anything. McEnroe was tennis's bad boy and Borg was the revered statesman, the anti-McEnroe. Many—if not most—in the crowd were screaming for the Swede to beat the New Yorker.

McEnroe heard, and had the will at that moment to dig in and play an extraordinary fifth set against a player who had won 14 straight fifth sets. He won the set, 6-4, won his second Open

title, and never again lost an important match to Borg—dethroning him at Wimbledon the next July, then beating him in the Open final again in September. Borg walked off the court that night and never played in another major tournament.

McEnroe won the Open once more—in 1984—beating Jimmy Connors in a classic five-set semifinal that stretched until nearly midnight before coming back the next day to wipe out Ivan Lendl in straight sets. Shortly after his '84 victory, the seventh and last of his Grand Slam titles, McEnroe wondered if he would ever be loved by the New York crowd. "Maybe when I'm older," he said. "Maybe when they think I'm vulnerable, they'll care about me."

As was often the case, McEnroe was prophetic. In 1990, he played the last of his great Open matches, a fourth-round match against Emilio Sanchez. McEnroe was 30, nearing the end of his career; Sanchez was a top ten player. Down two sets to one, it seemed McEnroe's Open farewell might come on a middle Sunday rather than on the last Sunday.

And then the crowd stepped in, almost willing McEnroe to victory, raising its decibel level at every key moment, refusing to allow McEnroe to lose.

He didn't. He walked off that night to an ovation louder than any he had received after his four Open championships. "Of all the great moments John had here, that one might have been his greatest," his younger brother Patrick said later. "Because that day, it wasn't just John out there, it was John and the entire stadium. It was a feeling he always wanted to have and, finally, he got it."

Yes, McEnroe got it. A champion. And now, a hero as well.

Where the stars come out

THE US OPEN IS A STAR-GAZERS paradise. For those two weeks each year when Flushing Meadows becomes the center of the sporting universe, there occurs a remarkable astrological phenomenon, as luminaries from the worlds of sports, entertainment, and politics gather in one place, creating a galaxy of stars unrivaled by anything this side of the outer stratosphere.

For this fortnight, the famous become the fans; box office titans cheering backhands, rock stars reveling in rallies; politicos–even presidents– engaged in court proceedings. They all are part of what makes the US Open one the world's greatest sports and entertainment spectaculars. On the courts; in the stands. There are stars everywhere you look. Telescope not required.

Martina
NAVRATILOVA

BY PETER BODO

NEW YORK HAS ALWAYS BEEN THE FOUNTAIN-head of America drama, so it is hardly surprising that the US Open has produced some of the most dramatic moments in tennis history. But among all the dramatis personae who have dominated the sport and left their distinct imprints on the US Open, none has done so with the signature—and often excruciating—flair of Martina Navratilova.

Who could have guessed that the great drama queen of sports in New York would be an aggressive, left-handed, tomboyish woman from a rural village in Czechoslovakia? Who would have suspected that Navratilova would put the words "US Open" on the lips of everyone from American presidents to Czech peasants long before she developed the game that would eventually earn her four titles at Flushing Meadows? In 1975, while she was just a plump, promising 17-year-old with a thick accent and untamed but arresting strokes, Navratilova lost a disappointingly one-sided US Open semifinal against the woman who would become her great career rival, Chris Evert. Critics noted that the already tempestuous Navratilova had rushed through the match like she had a train to catch, and in a way they were right. She had already chosen the fast track to freedom via defection, officially seeking political asylum in the U.S. the following morning after spending the night in hiding. "I had known from my very first trip to the U.S. in 1973 that I was born to be an American," she said.

And what an American Navratilova would become, evolving over the next few years into, arguably, the greatest woman

player of all time; the winner, ultimately, of eighteen Grand Slam singles titles. Yet Navratilova's history at Flushing Meadows was written in tears—tears of exultation, and tears of bitter disappointment. Tears of joy, and of frustration. This was one more way in which the unique contrast between Navratilova and her great rival and friend Evert was underscored.

Evert at the US Open defined perfection. But for Navratilova, the hard courts at Flushing Meadows radiated pressure and incertitude as intensely as they reflected the heat of the August sun. And great drama is always about imperfection. Check out Tracy Austin, beating Navratilova in 1981 in the first US Open title ever decided by a tie-breaker. It was a riveting, enervating, and shocking match, for by then Navratilova had won a number of Grand Slam titles, and she was heavily favored to triumph.

But the seeds of Narvatilova's deferred success also were sown in that match. As she once told me, "That was a really positive turning point for me and my history in New York. I wanted so much to be liked by the New York crowd, I was a regular Sally Field. And during that match, I finally felt the crowd turning toward me. I felt them more or less embrace me and say, 'Oh, we really like you.'"

Navratilova would electrify and surprise the crowd at Flushing Meadows for a number of years afterward. Eventually, the demons seemed quelled and the Sally Field issue had been laid to rest. In the city of the Great White Way, the crowd did not merely "like" Navratilova. They had grown to love her, and would continue to do so, for the drama she brought to their lives.

4th SET

Strokes of
Genius

The rectangular slabs of cement about the USTA National Tennis Center are professional tennis's ultimate proving grounds. No one has ever lucked their way to a US Open title. To win here, you need the whole package: intelligence, desire, stamina, courage. You need to own every shot in the book, and when that's not enough, you need to be ready to write a new chapter or two.

On these stages, you need to bring your best, hit your marks and, on more than a few occasions, pull off the impossible. Nothing can be left in reserve, or surely you will be left behind. You need to run faster, jump higher, stretch further. You'll need to dive on cement, when every shred of common sense within you reminds you of the perils of doing so. You can't care. It's about effort; about being willing—and able—to get to one more ball than that person across the net. Here, good just isn't good enough. You want to make your mark here, you've got to be sensational.

A leg up:
Martina Navratilova's serve-and-volley game (left) won her four US Open titles.

A singular focus:
Venus Williams (above) specializes in blurring an opponent's visions of greatness.

Don't try this at home:
Marat Safin (opposite) gets
inventive on the defensive.

Net results:
Stefan Edberg (above) won two
US Open crowns by making
countless impossible volleys.

Up in arms:
Elated fans (right) show their
excitement.

Best in show:
Michael Chang (above) has long been a champion retriever.

We have a winner: :
Arantxa Sanchez-Vicario (right) knows the thrill of victory.

Point well taken:
Jennifer Capriati (opposite) surges forward.

Rafter thought:
Aussie Patrick Rafter (right) always keeps his eyes on the prize.

The shadow knows:
Serena Williams (below) calls down thunder from a sunny sky.

Profiles in greatness:
Pete Sampras (opposite) has long specialized in superior service.

(Overleaf)
Flat-out fantastic:
Boris Becker goes horizontal in an effort to flag down an Ivan Lendl passing shot.

Ivan
LENDL

BY STEVE FLINK

H E WAS A CRAFTSMAN WHO HAD NO inclination to seek the emotional approval of his audiences. He was deadly serious about his profession, a champion who did not celebrate his fame, a private man performing earnestly yet sometimes uneasily in a public forum. Consequently, Ivan Lendl was never a popular figure at the US Open. The fans seldom showered this man with a warm reception when he went to work at his favorite hard court playground.

And yet, Lendl was worthy of much more admiration from those who watched him play during his salad days in New York. He produced a prodigious record at the USTA National Tennis Center. Of his 19 final-round appearances in Grand Slam events, a significant share took place at Flushing Meadows on a surface tailor-made for his groundbreaking, big-hitting, transformational game. He set a men's record unlikely to be surpassed by reaching eight title matches in a row. Beaten by Jimmy Connors in 1982-83 and ousted in 1984 by John McEnroe, Lendl garnered the crown from 1985-87 with final-round triumphs over McEnroe, Miloslav Mecir, and Mats Wilander. He would fall again at the last hurdle in bruising battles with Wilander and Boris Becker in 1988-89.

But what a remarkable run!

The defining moment for Lendl was his 1985 win over McEnroe. Lendl had handed McEnroe the most penetrating loss of the New Yorker's career in the 1984 French Open final. McEnroe retaliated emphatically in the US Open final three months later. Most astute observers looked for McEnroe to

prevail once more in 1985. Lendl, however, struck back boldly from 2-5 and set point down in the opening set to take apart his primary rival 7-6, 6-3, 6-4 with a signature display. At 25, in the heart of his prime, he blasted McEnroe off the court with the potency of his first serve, the crackle of his superb forehand, and the precision of his backhand passing shots.

That was a landmark victory for Lendl. It carried him inexorably through the next two years as he took over as the game's greatest player. He would take four more major titles in that span, and concluded his career with eight Grand Slam titles in his collection.

But it was Lendl's misfortune to be on the ascendancy while the charismatic McEnroe and Connors were moving slowly out of their primes. Inevitably, Open aficionados were drawn to those two dynamic Americans who ignited the crowds with the explosiveness of their expressions, from the positive to the profane.

Lendl, Czechoslovakian-born, established residence in the U.S. in 1984, becoming an American citizen eight years later. Nevertheless, the Open fans did not embrace him. He remained aloof in their estimation. Lendl was almost oblivious to how he was perceived; he simply got on with his business and played hard year after year until his retirement in 1994. Lendl taught a whole generation of top-flight players the essential value of discipline, unswerving commitment, and fitness with absolute focus. By leaving no stone unturned in his pursuit of big titles, Lendl reserved a place of honor for himself among the greatest players of his generation, and as one of the best of all time.

We have lift-off:
Yannick Noah (above) launches an all-out effort.

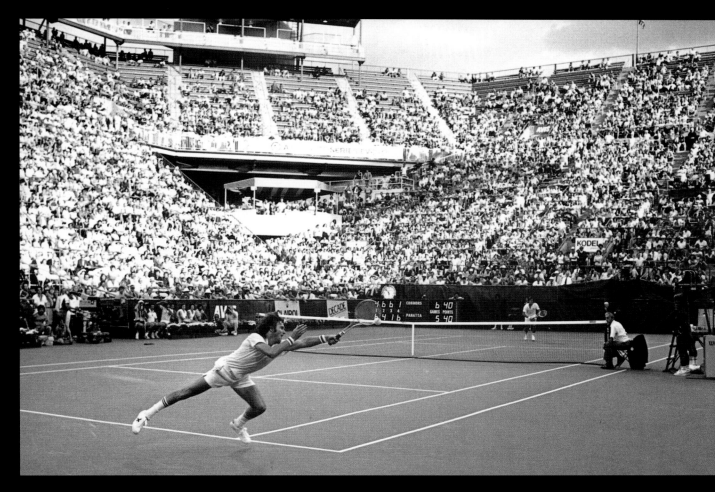

Without limits:
Jimmy Connors (top) stretches the boundaries of the court.

Twice as nice:
Pam Shriver and Martina Navratilova (above) prove their net worth.

Running down a dream:
Amelie Mauresmo (right) takes the tough shots in stride.

Great get:
James Blake (right) offers a backhanded compliment.

Just shoot me:
Photographers at the US Open (below) are nearly as plentiful as spectators.

A near miss:
Gabriela Sabatini (opposite) reacts to one that got away.

Mac attack:
John McEnroe (opposite) made his living—and his legend—at the net.

Muscling up:
Lleyton Hewitt (above) rips from the baseline.

Back to the future:
Up-and comer Andy Roddick (left) has shown an amazing knack for rising to every occasion.

Steffi GRAF

BY MARY CARILLO

NEW YORKERS LOVE HOT DOGS AND underdogs, and Steffi Graf was neither. What she was at the US Open for twelve straight years was this: strong-willed, fast, daring, nimble, commanding, intimidating. Yes, she played like that everywhere. But was there a better place than the hard courts of New York to show what she was made of? Was there a finer arena than the grand stage of Louis Armstrong Stadium for her to hit one of the great shots in tennis history—her poleax forehand? Through multiple injuries and traumas, Steffi Graf handled herself with uncommon dignity. She was just so damn tough. No wonder New Yorkers loved her.

That love affair started in 1985, when she played Pam Shriver in the quarterfinals. Down 1-4 in the third, Graf opened up her shoulders and went for winners. The quirky Grandstand fairly shook as Steffi passed Shriver, roared returns at her feet, stepped in and stepped up. It was a declaration of war on the whole joint.

The two best athletes in the sport— Graf and Martina Navratilova—played for a place in the final the following year. The epic ended deep in the third when a netted pass from Graf decided the third-set tie-break. It was tennis and tension of the highest order.

After losing the '87 final to Navratilova, Graf made 1988 her own. She entered Flushing Meadows with the first three legs of the Grand Slam; seven more matches and she'd win all four majors in a calendar year. She did it, of course, and since she was still in the mood, won the Olympics a few weeks later. The next year at the Open, she beat Navratilova in the final, clawing back from a set down and 4-2. The US Open trophy that year represented more

than a tournament win. Graf had become the world's very best.

This sort of dominance took massive effort. In the course of her career, Graf faced Chris Evert, Monica Seles, two major Martinas, and others like Arantxa Sanchez-Vicario and Gabriela Sabatini, all of whom demanded that she keep hammering away at the grand sculpture that is excellence. Graf was often injured, mostly in her legs, and yet her foot speed was rarely anything but astonishing. When she went for her forehand there was nothing reckless about it. You believed it would hit its mark. It almost always did.

But by the early '90s Monica Seles could attack even more fiercely than Graf. She took over the No. 1 ranking and was stabbed for it in 1993 by a demented Graf fan who wanted Steffi back on top. So when Seles and Graf played for the 1995 US Open Championship, the atmosphere was emotional beyond description. The match was uneven, so much was going through their minds: Seles, finally back where she belonged; Graf, relieved that Monica was back but still wanting the title for herself. Steffi prevailed in the end.

When Monica and Steffi met again the next year, the two were co-ranked No.1. Graf, burdened by her father's tax evasion troubles, played sloppy tennis throughout the fortnight. She won the final in straight sets anyway. So often she found a way to win.

Graf played one more US Open, losing in the fourth round in '98. Weeks before the '99 event, she announced her retirement. She came anyway, quietly watching Andre Agassi from an anonymous seat high in the stands. Andre won the title, and then won the girl. Steffi came away with something too often absent in her magnificent career—joy.

Sky-high overhead:
Pete Sampras (above) makes an opponent pay dearly for a short ball.

Over the line:
Boris Becker (right) earned his stripes in the attacking zone.

Alley cat:
Martina Hingis (below) goes wide for a winner.

Priming the pump:
Serena Williams (above) revels in her results.

Stick 'em up:
Marat Safin (right) surrenders to frustration.

Drawing a bead:
Venus Williams (opposite) has never allowed her goals to
exceed her reach.

(Overleaf)
Hair apparent:
The look may change, but through the years, Andre Agassi
has remained one to watch at the Open.

Pete
SAMPRAS

BY MARY CARILLO

PETE SAMPRAS WON HIS FIRST GRAND SLAM title at the US Open in 1990, and who did the 19-year-old beat to do it? Three-time US Open champion Ivan Lendl in the quarters. Four-time US Open champion John McEnroe in the semis. Andre Agassi in the final, winning on his 100th ace of the tournament. "I was unconscious," Sampras said of the run. "A pup going through the zone."

Still very much a boy in 1992, Sampras lost the US Open final to Stefan Edberg, and it was in the sleepless nights for months after the loss when Pete became a man, the one he always intended to be. "That loss really showed me that all these Slams are precious." he explained. Then he won eleven of his next twelve Grand Slam finals.

The US Open is Pete Sampras at his most vulnerable, the place where he's shown more of his heart, his humanity, his tennis mortality than anywhere else. He fell sick into the arms of his friend Vitas Gerulaitis after losing to the little known Jaime Yzaga in 1994. In many minds the winner of the 1995 US Open final between Sampras and Andre Agassi would decide which was the year's No. 1. At the end of the first set, with Agassi serving at 4-5, advantage Sampras, the two men put together one of the greatest points in tennis history. Every part of the game and every part of the court was used, and the two played one glorious shot after another in a 22-stroke sequence that drew the kind of raucous applause and cheering you can only hear in New York. When Sampras ended the rally with a winner and raised his arms in triumph, the fans not only felt

Pete's heat but saw his fire. He won the championship and ended the year at No. 1.

The next year, Sampras showed his guts in the truest sense, wretching and staggering in the quarterfinals as he fought off a match point and beat the Spaniard Alex Corretja 7-6 in the fifth. The tie-break included a lunge volley winner from Sampras that ruined match point for Corretja, a second serve ace to give himself a match point, and then— "not wanting to hit another ball," and not having to—a double fault from Alex ended it. A few days later, he beat Michael Chang in the final to earn his fourth US Open. After it ended, he looked into a television camera and spoke to his coach Tim Gullikson, who'd died earlier that year and who would have been 45 years old that day. "This one's for you, Gully," he said. "Happy Birthday."

In 1999, Sampras won Wimbledon for the sixth time, and back then it wasn't a good year for Pete unless he'd taken two majors. A herniated disc took Sampras out of the Open the day before it started. In 2000, the boy who'd won the US Open a decade earlier looked old and weary in the final against Marat Safin, and he was soundly beaten. His ambition and desire were still vivid in 2001, but after exceptional wins over Pat Rafter, Agassi, and Safin, he had little left to bring to the final against Lleyton Hewitt, and the match never got close. Still, he plays on.

This US Open Championship has matured Sampras—and has aged him, too. It's Pete's most emotional major, the one that made him who he is, the one that made us care about him.

5thSET

Courting
Fame

Everything about the US Open is hard, from the courts upward. Breaking points far outweigh breaks. The world's toughest tennis is played here on these courts. Only the strong survive. But should you somehow, some way, win seven matches over the course of this fabulous fortnight, you get a trophy, a very large paycheck, and credentials that last a lifetime.

There is no feeling quite like it, no words more impressive on a résumé than "US Open champion." Very few know that feeling, if only because so few have the means to lift themselves into that rarified air. Seven matches may not seem like all that much, but seven matches in the heat of the New York summer, before the world's most demanding fans, against the world's greatest players is this sport's ultimate test. When you've passed it, you are a champion in the truest sense of the word.

Applause, applause:
Andy Roddick (left) salutes his fans as he exits the stage.

Crowd a-peel:
Andre Agassi (above) proves willing to give his fans the shirt off his back.

On top of the world:
Aussie Lleyton Hewitt (opposite) revels in the thrill of a US Open title.

Sky high:
Stefan Edberg (left) soars on the wings of victory.

Bravo, Boris:
A beaming Boris Becker (below) brightens the evening at Flushing Meadows.

Thanksgiving Day:
Martina Navratilova (below, left) offers thanks to a higher authority.

Andre AGASSI

BY PETER BODO

TO MANY GREAT PLAYERS, THE US OPEN has been like an imposing, muscular, and spirited, if inanimate, sibling. They grew up with it, becoming comfortable with the outsized personality of the event. But Andre Agassi is different. Agassi did not grow up *with* the US Open. He grew up *at* it. And that places this man—and this ultimately manhandling event—into a unique relationship.

In 1988, on the grand stage of Louis Armstrong Stadium, 18-year-old Agassi, wearing something more like a costume than tennis kit, his face barely visible amid all that wild, bleached hair, took his sledgehammer ground strokes to the game of U.S. tennis icon Jimmy Connors in the quarterfinals.

When the 6-1, 6-1, 6-2 demolition was over, when Connors's game lay in busted pieces on the stadium floor, the callow Agassi said no, the scores were not surprising to him at all—he had *expected* to win by that wide a margin.

It looked then as if this showman from Las Vegas would flat-out *own* the Open the way his smoldering victim once had. Of course, it didn't work out that way. Things—and we are not talking about male pattern baldness—got in the way. Agassi soon began to experience a deep ambivalence toward the game. He showed a surprising, inner gentleness that does not always play well in hardened New York. Instead of reveling in his status as barbarian warrior from the ancient land of Neon, he seemed to shrink from it.

In 1994, still just 24, Agassi is already a strong candidate for tennis's Lifetime Underachievement Award, having collected but one Grand Slam title in his career. He is dealing

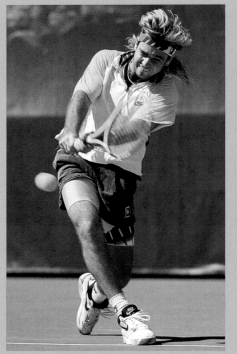

with the sobering realities of a career-threatening wrist injury. At the US Open, a skeptical media has written him off as a lightweight, and Agassi is off the radar screen in every possible way—not even seeded at this most demanding of all tennis tournaments. *Nobody* expected what happened next. Point-by-point, game-by-game, set-by-set, match-by-excruciating match, Agassi endured a trial-by-fire while undergoing a startling transformation. No less improbably, he was shepherded along the road of renewal with the compassion, sympathy, and encouragement of a New York crowd that has rarely been described as "nurturing."

It was as if the crowd collectively set aside the binoculars, ceased trying to figure out who Trump was sitting with, and settled in to take a genuine, vested interest as a less protean Andre finally began to materialize out of the smoke and lasers and mirrors. What really happened was quite simple: in the course of becoming the first unseeded champion at the tournament in the Open era, Andre Agassi grew up. "After I injured my wrist I was overcome by this fear that my career might be over," Agassi once told me. "I was afraid that I might never truly know how good I could be. That's what the Open of 1994 was about for me—a day of reckoning."

Since then, *because* of then, Agassi now owns the hearts of the New York crowd, which cuts right to the point. What New Yorkers most love is not people, but story. They are addicted to narrative, and in this place, a showman found substance, giving them one of the best Coming of Age stories ever told in sports—a story he continues to embellish.

Helping hands:
Crowd favorite Todd Martin (above) shares the glory with his supporters.

Taking flight:
Martina Hingis (opposite) knows the rarified air in which US Open champions dwell.

A grand exit:
Zina Garrison and Chris Evert (above) share an emotional moment after Garrison defeated Evert in her last US Open match.

Sealed with a kiss:
Stan Smith (left) shows appreciation for the tools of his trade.

Unflagging appeal:
Monica Seles (opposite) is a portrait of delight during the trophy presentation.

Venus WILLIAMS

BY JOEL DRUCKER

THE ASCENT OF VENUS EBONE STARR Williams, along with her younger sister Serena, speaks volumes about the growth of the US Open. The sedate, garden party days of Forest Hills have blossomed into technicolor glitz and glamour. Thanks to players like Venus, the contemporary US Open has become both big-time sports and high-octane popular culture. In the spirit of Jimmy Connors, Arthur Ashe, Andre Agassi, and Billie Jean King, she has been a Pied Piper, drawing millions of new fans to tennis, in no small part due to her performances on the grand stage of Flushing Meadows.

Willowy yet powerful, mature yet impassioned, Venus in fact treats the world as her stage. But whether she's sporting beads or showcasing dresses, smacking a forehand or cracking a smile, laughing with Serena or chatting up Bill Clinton, Venus lives for the spotlight only the US Open can provide. A generator of headlines benign and controversial, Williams has proven that at heart she wants to be remembered not strictly as a star but also as a champion.

Williams's fighting spirit was apparent from her debut at the US Open in 1997, the same year that saw the inauguration of Arthur Ashe Stadium. She'd arrived in New York by way of the rough-and-tumble streets of Compton, California. Her father, Richard, had dubbed her the "Cinderella of the ghetto." But in the semis of that rookie campaign, Irina Spirlea threatened to turn Cinderella into a pumpkin when she held two match points against Venus in a third-set tiebreak. Pressed deep into her backhand corner, Venus responded with one of the greatest shots in US Open history—a sizzling down-the-line winner. Minutes later, she was in the final. Though she'd lose that match to Martina Hingis, it was clear Venus was ready to commence a notable New York run.

Never was the depth of Venus's emotional commitment more vivid than at the 1999 US Open. Having lost a painfully close semifinal to Hingis, she dutifully watched Serena win the tournament. It had always seemed inevitable that Venus, the older sibling, would be the first to know that singular feeling of Grand Slam glory. But the site of Venus numbly watching her sister take the prize was jarring—and, as time would tell, profoundly motivational.

The next year, Venus came to New York with renewed purpose, and would earn the first of two straight US Open titles with a game equal parts firepower and flair.

Her speed and power, coupled with her will and intelligence, have made her a formidable competitor. Covering the court like a gazelle, bearing down on big points, striking high-speed serves, Williams is the most dangerous of opponents: equally comfortable on defense and offense, always determined to strike the best possible shot, unwilling to back off, capable of the spectacular and just as capable of making the spectacular seem routine.

In her 2001 final-round victory over Serena, joy and poise carried the day on an evening that was a watershed for both tennis and the Williams family. A prime-time, Saturday night, sister-to-sister final, broadcast nationally, was a tennis first. For the sisters, doubles partners and best friends, it was a grand moment in an odyssey still in its early stages. And for Venus, another coronation. Cinderella has indeed become the Queen.

One moment in time:
Lindsay Davenport (left) exults in victory.

Unmatched:
Jimmy Connors (opposite) is the personification of the energy and excitement unique to the US Open.

MEN'S SINGLES

Year	Champion	Runner-up	Score
1881	Richard D. Sears	William E. Glyn	6-0, 6-3, 6-2
1882	Richard D. Sears	Clarence M. Clark	6-1, 6-4, 6-0
1883	Richard D. Sears	James Dwight	6-2, 6-0, 9-7
1884	Richard D. Sears	Howard A. Taylor	6-0, 1-6, 6-0, 6-2
1885	Richard D. Sears	Godfrey M. Brinley	6-3, 4-6, 6-0, 6-3
1886	Richard D. Sears	R. Livingston Beeckman	4-6, 6-1, 6-3, 6-4
1887	Richard D. Sears	Henry W. Slocum, Jr.	6-1, 6-3, 6-2
1888	Henry W. Slocum, Jr.	Howard A. Taylor	6-4, 6-1, 6-0
1889	Henry W. Slocum, Jr	Quincy Shaw	6-3, 6-1, 4-6, 6-2
1890	Oliver S. Campbell	Henry W. Slocum, Jr.	6-2, 4-6, 6-3, 6-1
1891	Oliver S. Campbell	Clarence Hobart	2-6, 7-5, 7-9, 6-1, 6-2
1892	Oliver S. Campbell	Fred H. Hovey	7-5, 3-6, 6-3, 7-5
1893	Robert D. Wrenn	Fred H. Hovey	6-4, 3-6, 6-4, 6-4
1894	Robert D. Wrenn	Manliff Goodbody	6-8, 6-1, 6-4, 6-4
1895	Fred H. Hovey	Robert D. Wrenn	6-3, 6-2, 6-4
1896	Robert D. Wrenn	Fred H. Hovey	7-5, 3-6, 6-0, 1-6, 6-1
1897	Robert D. Wrenn	Wilberforce Eaves	4-6, 8-6, 6-3, 2-6, 6-2
1898	Malcolm D. Whitman	Dwight F. Davis	3-6, 6-2, 6-2, 6-1
1899	Malcolm D. Whitman	J. Parmly Paret	6-1, 6-2, 3-6, 7-5
1900	Malcolm D. Whitman	William A. Larned	6-4, 1-6, 6-2, 6-2
1901	William A. Larned	Beals C. Wright	6-2, 6-8, 6-4, 6-4
1902	William A. Larned	Reginald F. Doherty	4-6, 6-2, 6-4, 8-6
1903	Hugh L. Doherty	William A. Larned	6-0, 6-3, 10-8
1904	Holcombe Ward	William J. Clothier	10-8, 6-4, 9-7
1905	Beals C. Wright	Holcombe Ward	6-2, 6-1, 11-9
1906	William A. Larned	Beals C. Wright	6-3, 6-0, 6-4
1907	William A. Larned	Robert LeRoy	6-2, 6-2, 6-4
1908	William A. Larned	Beals C. Wright	6-1, 6-2, 8-6
1909	William A. Larned	William J. Clothier	6-1, 6-2, 5-7, 1-6, 6-1
1910	William A. Larned	Thomas C. Bundy	6-1, 5-7, 6-0, 6-8, 6-1
1911	William A. Larned	Maurice E. McLoughlin	6-4, 6-4, 6-2
1912	Maurice E. McLoughlin	Wallace F. Johnson	3-6, 2-6, 6-2, 6-4, 6-2
1913	Maurice E. McLoughlin	R. Norris Williams	6-4, 5-7, 6-3, 6-1
1914	R. Norris Williams	Maurice E. McLoughlin	6-3, 8-6, 10-8
1915	William M. Johnston	Maurice E. McLoughlin	1-6, 6-0, 7-5, 10-8
1916	R. Norris Williams	William M. Johnston	4-6, 6-4, 0-6, 6-2, 6-4
1917	R. Lindley Murray	Nathaniel W. Niles	5-7, 8-6, 6-3, 6-3
1918	R. Lindley Murray	William T. Tilden	6-3, 6-1, 7-5
1919	William M. Johnston	William T. Tilden	6-4, 6-4, 6-3
1920	William T. Tilden	William M. Johnston	6-1, 1-6, 7-5, 5-7, 6-3
1921	William T. Tilden	William M. Johnston	6-1, 6-3, 6-1
1922	William T. Tilden	William M. Johnston	4-6, 3-6, 6-2, 6-3, 6-4
1923	William T. Tilden	William M. Johnston	6-4, 6-1, 6-4
1924	William T. Tilden	William M. Johnston	6-1, 9-7, 6-2
1925	William T. Tilden	William M. Johnston	4-6, 11-9, 6-3, 4-6, 6-3
1926	Rene Lacoste	Jean Borotra	6-4, 6-0, 6-4
1927	Rene Lacoste	William T. Tilden	11-9, 6-3, 11-9
1928	Henri Cochet	Francis T. Hunter	4-6, 6-4, 3-6, 7-5, 6-3
1929	William T. Tilden	Francis T. Hunter	3-6, 6-3, 4-6, 6-2, 6-4
1930	John H. Doeg	Francis X. Shields	10-8, 1-6, 6-4, 16-14
1931	H. Ellsworth Vines	George M. Lott, Jr.	7-9, 6-3, 9-7, 7-5
1932	H. Ellsworth Vines	Henri Cochet	6-4, 6-4, 6-4
1933	Fred Perry	John H. Crawford	6-3, 11-13, 4-6, 6-0, 6-1
1934	Fred Perry	Wilmer L. Allison	6-4, 6-3, 1-6, 8-6
1935	Wilmer L. Allison	Sidney B. Wood	6-2, 6-2, 6-3
1936	Fred Perry	J. Donald Budge	2-6, 6-2, 8-6, 1-6, 10-8
1937	J. Donald Budge	B. Gottfried von Cramm	6-1, 7-9, 6-1, 3-6, 6-1
1938	J. Donald Budge	C. Gene Mako	6-3, 6-8 6-2, 6-1
1939	Robert L. Riggs	S. Welby van Horn	6-4, 6-2, 6-4
1940	W. Donald McNeill	Robert L. Riggs	4-6, 6-8, 6-3, 6-3, 7-5
1941	Robert L. Riggs	Francis Kovacs, 2d	5-7, 6-1, 6-3, 6-3
1942	Frederick R. Schroeder, Jr.	Frank A. Parker	8-6, 7-5, 3-6, 4-6, 6-2
1943	Lt. Joseph R. Hunt	Seaman Jack Kramer	6-3, 6-8, 10-8, 6-0
1944	Sgt. Frank A. Parker	William F. Talbert	6-4, 3-6, 6-3, 6-3
1945	Sgt. Frank A. Parker	William F. Talbert	14-12, 6-1, 6-2
1946	Jack Kramer	Thomas P. Brown, Jr.	9-7, 6-3, 6-0
1947	Jack Kramer	Frank A. Parker	4-6, 2-6, 6-1, 6-0, 6-3
1948	Richard A. "Pancho" Gonzales	Eric W. Sturgess	6-2, 6-3, 14-12
1949	Richard A. "Pancho" Gonzales	F.R. Schroeder, Jr.	16-18, 2-6, 6-1, 6-2, 6-4
1950	Arthur Larsen	Herbert Flam	6-3, 4-6, 5-7, 6-4, 6-3
1951	Frank Sedgman	E. Victor Seixas, Jr.	6-4, 6-1, 6-1
1952	Frank Sedgman	Gardnar Mulloy	6-1, 6-2, 6-3
1953	Tony Trabert	E. Victor Seixas, Jr.	6-3, 6-2, 6-3
1954	E. Victor Seixas, Jr.	Rex Hartwig	3-6, 6-2, 6-4, 6-4
1955	Tony Trabert	Kenneth Rosewall	9-7 6-3, 6-3
1956	Kenneth Rosewall	Lewis Hoad	4-6, 6-2, 6-3, 6-3
1957	Malcolm J. Anderson	Ashley J. Cooper	10-8, 7-5, 6-4
1958	Ashley J. Cooper	Malcolm J. Anderson	6-2, 3-6, 4-6, 10-8, 8-6
1959	Neale Fraser	Alejandro "Alex" Olmedo	6-3, 5-7, 6-2, 6-4
1960	Neale Fraser	Rod Laver	6-4, 6-4, 9-7
1961	Roy Emerson	Rod Laver	7-5, 6-3, 6-2
1962	Rod Laver	Roy Emerson	6-2, 6-4, 5-7, 6-4
1963	Rafael Osuna	Frank Froehling, III	7-5, 6-4, 6-2
1964	Roy Emerson	Fred Stolle	6-4, 6-2, 6-4
1965	Manuel Santana	Cliff Drysdale	6-2, 7-9, 7-5, 6-1
1966	Fred Stolle	John Newcombe	4-6, 12-10, 6-3, 6-4
1967	John Newcombe	Clark Graebner	6-4, 6-4, 8-6
1968*	Arthur Ashe	Bob Lutz	4-6, 6-3, 8-10, 6-0, 6-4

Open Era

Year	Champion	Runner-up	Score
1968*	Arthur Ashe	Tom Okker	14-12, 5-7, 6-3, 3-6, 6-3
1969	Rodney Laver	Tony Roche	7-9, 6-1, 6-2, 6-2
1970	Kenneth Rosewall	Tony Roche	2-6, 6-4, 7-6, 6-3
1971	Stan Smith	Jan Kodes	3-6, 6-3, 6-2, 7-6
1972	Ilie Nastase	Arthur Ashe	3-6, 6-3, 6-7, 6-4, 6-3
1973	John Newcombe	Jan Kodes	6-4, 1-6, 4-6, 6-2, 6-2
1974	Jimmy Connors	Kenneth Rosewall	6-1, 6-0, 6-1
1975	Manuel Orantes	Jimmy Connors	6-4, 6-3, 6-3
1976	Jimmy Connors	Bjorn Borg	6-4, 3-6, 7-6, 6-4
1977	Guillermo Vilas	Jimmy Connors	2-6, 6-3, 7-5, 6-0
1978	Jimmy Connors	Bjorn Borg	6-4, 6-2, 6-2
1979	John McEnroe	Vitas Gerulaitis	7-5, 6-3, 6-3
1980	John McEnroe	Bjorn Borg	7-6, 6-1, 6-7, 5-7, 6-4
1981	John McEnroe	Bjorn Borg	4-6, 6-2, 6-4, 6-3
1982	Jimmy Connors	Ivan Lendl	6-3, 6-2, 4-6, 6-4
1983	Jimmy Connors	Ivan Lendl	6-3, 6-7, 7-5, 6-0
1984	John McEnroe	Ivan Lendl	6-3, 6-4, 6-1
1985	Ivan Lendl	John McEnroe	7-6, 6-3, 6-4
1986	Ivan Lendl	Miloslav Mecir	6-4, 6-2, 6-0
1987	Ivan Lendl	Mats Wilander	6-7, 6-0, 7-6, 6-4
1988	Mats Wilander	Ivan Lendl	6-4, 4-6, 6-3, 5-7, 6-4
1989	Boris Becker	Ivan Lendl	7-6, 1-6, 6-3, 7-6
1990	Pete Sampras	Andre Agassi	6-4, 6-3, 6-2
1991	Stefan Edberg	Jim Courier	6-2, 6-4, 6-0
1992	Stefan Edberg	Pete Sampras	3-6, 6-4, 7-6, 6-2
1993	Pete Sampras	Cedric Pioline	6-4, 6-4, 6-3
1994	Andre Agassi	Michael Stich	6-1, 7-6, 7-5
1995	Pete Sampras	Andre Agassi	6-4, 6-3, 4-6, 7-5
1996	Pete Sampras	Michael Chang	6-1, 6-4, 7-6
1997	Patrick Rafter	Greg Rusedski	6-3, 6-2, 4-6, 7-5
1998	Patrick Rafter	Mark Philippoussis	6-3, 3-6, 6-2, 6-0
1999	Andre Agassi	Todd Martin	6-4, 6-7, 6-7, 6-3, 6-2
2000	Marat Safin	Pete Sampras	6-4, 6-3, 6-3
2001	Lleyton Hewitt	Pete Sampras	7-6, 6-1, 6-1

WOMEN'S SINGLES

Year	Champion	Runner-up	Score
1887	Ellen Hansell	Laura Knight	6-1, 6-0
1888	Bertha L. Townsend	Ellen Hansell	6-3, 6-5
1889	Bertha L. Townsend	Lida D. Voorhes	7-5, 6-2
1890	Ellen C. Roosevelt	Bertha L. Townsend	6-2, 6-2
1891	Mabel Cahill	Ellen C. Roosevelt	6-4, 6-1, 4-6, 6-3
1892	Mabel Cahill	Elisabeth Moore	5-7, 6-3, 6-4, 4-6, 6-2
1893	Aline Terry	Augusta Schultz	6-1, 6-3
1894	Helen Hellwig	Aline Terry	7-5, 3-6, 6-0, 3-6, 6-3
1895	Juliette Atkinson	Helen Hellwig	6-4, 6-2, 6-1
1896	Elisabeth Moore	Juliette Atkinson	6-4, 4-6, 6-2, 6-2
1897	Juliette Atkinson	Elisabeth Moore	6-3, 6-3, 4-6, 3-6, 6-3
1898	Juliette Atkinson	Marion Jones	6-3, 5-7, 6-4, 2-6, 7-5
1899*	Marion Jones	Maud Banks	6-1, 6-1, 7-5
1900*	Myrtle McAteer	Edith Parker	6-2, 6-2, 6-0
1901	Elisabeth Moore	Myrtle McAteer	6-4, 3-6, 7-5, 2-6, 6-2
1902	Marion Jones	Elisabeth Moore	6-1, 1-0 ret.
1903	Elisabeth Moore	Marion Jones	7-5, 8-6
1904	May Sutton	Elisabeth Moore	6-1, 6-2

Champions

Year	Champion	Runner-up	Score
1905*	Elisabeth Moore	Helen Homans	6-4, 5-7, 6-1
1906*	Helen Homans	Maud Barger-Wallach	6-4, 6-3
1907*	Evelyn Sears	Carrie B. Neely	6-3, 6-2
1908	Maud Barger-Wallach	Evelyn Sears	6-3, 1-6, 6-3
1909	Hazel V. Hotchkiss	Maud Barger-Wallach	6-0, 6-1
1910	Hazel V. Hotchkiss	Louise Hammond	6-4, 6-2
1911	Hazel V. Hotchkiss	Florence Sutton	8-10, 6-1, 9-7
1912	Mary K. Browne	Eleonora Sears	6-4, 6-2
1913	Mary K. Browne	Dorothy Green	6-2, 7-5
1914	Mary K. Browne	Marie Wagner	6-2, 1-6, 6-1
1915	Molla Bjurstedt	H. Hotchkiss Wightman	4-6, 6-2, 6-0
1916	Molla Bjurstedt	L. Hammond Raymond	6-0, 6-1
1917	Molla Bjurstedt	Marion Vanderhoef	4-6, 6-0, 6-2
1918	Molla Bjurstedt	Eleanor E. Goss	6-4, 6-3
1919	Hazel Hotchkiss Wightman	Marion Zinderstein	6-1, 6-2
1920	Molla B. Mallory	Marion Zinderstein	6-3, 6-1
1921	Molla B. Mallory	Mary K. Browne	4-6, 6-4, 6-2
1922	Molla B. Mallory	Helen Wills	6-3, 6-1
1923	Helen Wills	Molla B. Mallory	6-2, 6-1
1924	Helen Wills	Molla B. Mallory	6-1, 6-3
1925	Helen Wills	Kathleen "Kitty" McKane	3-6, 6-0, 6-2
1926	Molla B. Mallory	Elizabeth Ryan	4-6, 6-4, 9-7
1927	Helen Wills	Betty Nuthall	6-1, 6-4
1928	Helen Wills	Helen H. Jacobs	6-2, 6-1
1929	Helen Wills	Phoebe Holcroft Watson	6-4, 6-2
1930	Betty Nuthall	Anna McCune Harper	6-1, 6-4
1931	Helen Wills Moody	Eileen B. Whitingstall	6-4, 6-1
1932	Helen H. Jacobs	Carolin A. Babcock	6-2, 6-2
1933	Helen H. Jacobs	Helen Wills Moody	8-6, 3-6, 3-0 ret.
1934	Helen H. Jacobs	Sarah H. Palfrey	6-1, 6-4
1935	Helen H. Jacobs	Sarah Palfrey Fabyan	6-2, 6-4
1936	Alice Marble	Helen H. Jacobs	4-6, 6-3, 6-2
1937	Anita Lizana	Jadwiga Jedrzejowska	6-4, 6-2
1938	Alice Marble	Nancye Wynne	6-0, 6-3
1939	Alice Marble	Helen H. Jacobs	6-0, 8-10, 6-4
1940	Alice Marble	Helen H. Jacobs	6-2, 6-3
1941	Sarah Palfrey Cooke	Pauline Betz	7-5, 6-2
1942	Pauline Betz	A. Louise Brough	4-6, 6-1, 6-4
1943	Pauline Betz	A. Louise Brough	6-3, 5-7, 6-3
1944	Pauline Betz	Margaret E. Osborne	6-3, 8-6
1945	Sarah Palfrey Cooke	Pauline Betz	3-6, 8-6, 6-4
1946	Pauline Betz	Doris Hart	11-9, 6-3
1947	A. Louise Brough	Margaret E. Osborne	8-6, 4-6, 6-1
1948	Margaret Osborne duPont	A. Louise Brough	4-6, 6-4, 15-13
1949	Margaret Osborne duPont	Doris Hart	6-4, 6-1
1950	Margaret Osborne duPont	Doris Hart	6-3, 6-3
1951	Maureen Connolly	Shirley J. Fry	6-3, 1-6, 6-4
1952	Maureen Connolly	Doris Hart	6-3, 7-5
1953	Maureen Connolly	Doris Hart	6-2, 6-4
1954	Doris Hart	A. Louise Brough	6-8, 6-1, 8-6
1955*	Doris Hart	Patricia Ward	6-4, 6-2
1956	Shirley J. Fry	Althea Gibson	6-3, 6-4
1957	Althea Gibson	A. Louise Brough	6-3, 6-2
1958	Althea Gibson	Darlene R. Hard	3-6, 6-1, 6-2
1959	Maria Bueno	Christine Truman	6-1, 6-4
1960	Darlene R. Hard	Maria Bueno	6-4, 10-12, 6-4
1961	Darlene R. Hard	Ann Haydon	6-3, 6-4
1962	Margaret Smith	Darlene R. Hard	9-7, 6-4
1963	Maria Bueno	Margaret Smith	7-5, 6-4
1964	Maria Bueno	C. Caldwell Graebner	6-1, 6-0
1965	Margaret Smith	Billie Jean Moffitt	8-6, 7-5
1966	Maria Bueno	Nancy Richey	6-3, 6-1
1967	Billie Jean King	Ann Haydon Jones	11-9, 6-4
1968*	Margaret Smith Court	Maria Bueno	6-2, 6-2
Open Era			
1968*	Virginia Wade	Billie Jean King	6-4, 6-4
1969	Margaret Smith Court	Nancy Richey	6-2, 6-2
1970	Margaret Smith Court	Rosemary Casals	6-2, 2-6, 6-1
1971	Billie Jean King	Rosemary Casals	6-4, 7-6
1972	Billie Jean King	Kerry Melville	6-3, 7-5
1973	Margaret Smith Court	Evonne Goolagong	7-6, 5-7, 6-2
1974	Billie Jean King	Evonne Goolagong	3-6, 6-3, 7-5
1975	Chris Evert	Evonne Goolagong	5-7, 6-4, 6-2
1976	Chris Evert	Evonne Goolagong	6-3, 6-0
1977	Chris Evert	Wendy Turnbull	7-6, 6-2
1978	Chris Evert	Pam Shriver	7-5, 6-4
1979	Tracy Austin	Chris Evert Lloyd	6-4, 6-3
1980	Chris Evert Lloyd	Hana Mandlikova	5-7, 6-1, 6-1
1981	Tracy Austin	Martina Navratilova	1-6, 7-6, 7-6
1982	Chris Evert Lloyd	Hana Mandlikova	6-3, 6-1
1983	Martina Navratilova	Chris Evert Lloyd	6-1, 6-3
1984	Martina Navratilova	Chris Evert Lloyd	4-6, 6-4, 6-4
1985	Hana Mandlikova	Martina Navratilova	7-6, 1-6, 7-6
1986	Martina Navratilova	Helena Sukova	6-3, 6-2
1987	Martina Navratilova	Steffi Graf	7-6, 6-1
1988	Steffi Graf	Gabriela Sabatini	6-3, 3-6, 6-1
1989	Steffi Graf	Martina Navratilova	3-6, 7-5, 6-1
1990	Gabriela Sabatini	Steffi Graf	6-2, 7-6
1991	Monica Seles	Martina Navratilova	7-6, 6-1
1992	Monica Seles	Arantxa Sanchez-Vicario	6-3, 6-3
1993	Steffi Graf	Helena Sukova	6-3, 6-3
1994	Arantxa Sanchez-Vicario	Steffi Graf	1-6, 7-6, 6-4
1995	Steffi Graf	Monica Seles	7-6, 0-6, 6-3
1996	Steffi Graf	Monica Seles	7-5, 6-4
1997	Martina Hingis	Venus Williams	6-0, 6-4
1998	Lindsay Davenport	Martina Hingis	6-3, 7-5
1999	Serena Williams	Martina Hingis	6-3, 7-6
2000	Venus Williams	Lindsay Davenport	6-4, 7-5
2001	Venus Williams	Serena Williams	6-2, 6-4

* Year in which both amateur and professional events were held.

MEN'S DOUBLES

Year	Champions	Runners-up	Score
1881	Clarence M. Clark – F.W. Taylor	A.E. Newbold – A. Van Rensselaer	6-5, 6-4, 6-5
1882	J. Dwight – R.D. Sears	C. Nightingale – G.M. Smith	6-2, 6-4, 6-4
1883	J. Dwight – R.D. Sears	A.E. Newbold – A. Van Rensselaer	6-0, 6-2, 6-2
1884	James Dwight – R.D. Sears	W.V.R. Berry – A. Van Rensselaer	6-4, 6-1, 8-10, 6-4
1885	J.S. Clark – R.D. Sears	W.P. Knapp – H.W. Slocum, Jr	6-3, 6-0, 6-2
1886	James Dwight – R.D. Sears	G.M. Brinley – H.A. Taylor	7-5, 5-7, 7-5, 6-4
1887	James Dwight – R.D. Sears	H.W. Slocum, Jr. – H.A. Taylor	6-4, 3-6, 2-6, 6-3, 6-3
1888	O.S. Campbell – V.G. Hall	Clarence Hobart – E.P. Macmullen	6-4, 6-2, 6-4
1889	H.W. Slocum, Jr. – H.A. Taylor	O.S. Campbell – V.G. Hall	6-1, 6-3, 6-2
1890	V.G. Hall – C. Hobart	C. Carver – J. Ryerson	6-3, 4-6, 6-2, 2-6, 6-3
1891	O.S. Campbell – R. Huntington, Jr.	V.G. Hall – C. Hobart	6-3, 6-4, 8-6
1892	O.S. Campbell – R. Huntington, Jr.	Edward L. Hall – V.G. Hall	6-4, 6-2, 4-6, 6-3
1893	C. Hobart – F.H. Hovey	O.S. Campbell – R. Huntington, Jr.	6-3, 6-4, 4-6, 6-2
1894	C. Hobart – F.H. Hovey	Carr B. Neel – Samuel R. Neel	6-3, 8-6, 6-1
1895	M.G. Chace – R.D. Wrenn	Clarence Hobart – Fred H. Hovey	7-5, 6-1, 8-6
1896	C.B. Neel – G.P. Sheldon, Jr.	Malcolm G. Chace – R.D. Wrenn	6-3, 1-6, 6-1, 3-6, 6-1
1897	G.P. Sheldon, Jr. – L.E. Ware	Harold S. Mahony – H.A. Nisbet	11-13, 6-2, 9-7, 1-6, 6-1
1898	G.P. Sheldon, Jr. – L.E. Ware	Dwight F. Davis – Holcombe Ward	1-6, 7-5, 6-4, 4-6, 7-5
1899	D.F. Davis – H. Ward	George P. Sheldon, Jr. – L.E. Ware	6-4, 6-4, 6-3
1900	D.F. Davis – H. Ward	Fred B. Alexander – R.D. Little	6-4, 9-7, 12-10
1901	D.F. Davis – H. Ward	Leo E. Ware – Beals C. Wright	6-3, 9-7, 6-1
1902	H.L. Doherty – R.F. Doherty	Dwight F. Davis – Holcombe Ward	11-9, 12-10, 6-4
1903	H.L. Doherty – R. F. Doherty	Kreigh Collins – L. Harry Waidner	7-5, 6-3, 6-3
1904	H. Ward – Beals C. Wright	Kreigh Collins – Raymond D. Little	1-6, 6-2, 3-6, 6-4, 6-1
1905	H. Ward – Beals C. Wright	Fred B. Alexander – H.H. Hackett	6-4, 6-4, 6-1
1906	H. Ward – Beals C. Wright	Fred B. Alexander – H.H. Hackett	6-3, 3-6, 6-3, 6-3
1907	F.B. Alexander – H.H. Hackett	B.M. Grant – Nat Thornton	6-2, 6-1, 6-1
1908	F.B. Alexander – H.H. Hackett	Raymond D. Little – B.C. Wright	6-1, 7-5, 6-2
1909	F.B. Alexander – H.H. Hackett	George J. Janes – M.E. McLoughlin	6-4, 6-4, 6-0
1910	F.B. Alexander – H.H. Hackett	Thomas C. Bundy – T. W. Hendrick	6-1, 86- 6-3
1911	R. D. Little – G. F. Touchard	F. B. Alexander – Harold H. Hackett	7-5, 13-15, 6-2, 6-4
1912	T.C. Bundy – M.E. McLoughlin	Raymond D. Little – G.F. Touchard	3-6, 6-2, 6-1, 7-5
1913	T.C. Bundy – M.E. McLoughlin	Clarence J. Griffin – J.R. Strachan	6-4, 7-5, 6-1
1914	T.C. Bundy – M.E. McLoughlin	George M. Church – Dean Mathey	6-4, 6-2, 6-4
1915	C. Griffin – W. M. Johnston	T.C. Bundy – M.E. McLoughlin	2-6, 6-3, 6-4, 3-6, 6-3
1916	C. Griffin – W. M. Johnston	Ward Dawson – M.E. McLoughlin	6-4, 6-3, 5-7, 6-3
1917	F.B. Alexander – H. Throckmorton	Harry C. Johnson – Irving C. Wright	11-9, 6-4, 6-4
1918	V. Richards – W.T. Tilden	Fred B. Alexander – B.C. Wright	6-3, 6-4, 3-6, 2-6, 6-2
1919	N.E. Brookes – G.L. Patterson	V. Richards – William T. Tilden	8-6, 6-3, 4-6, 4-6, 6-2
1920	C. Griffin – W.M. Johnston	Willis F. Davis – Roland E. Roberts	6-2, 6-2, 6-3
1921	V. Richards – W. T. Tilden	W. Washburn – R. N. Williams	13-11, 12-10, 6-1
1922	V. Richards – W. T. Tilden	Pat O'Hara Wood – G. L. Patterson	4-6, 6-1, 6-3, 6-4
1923	B.I.C. Norton – W.T. Tilden	W. Washburn – R. N. Williams	3-6, 6-2, 6-3, 5-7, 6-2
1924	H. Kinsey – Robert Kinsey	Pat O'Hara Wood – G. L. Patterson	7-5, 5-7, 7-9, 6-3, 6-4
1925	V. Richards – R.N. Williams	John B. Hawkes – G. L. Patterson	6-2, 8-10, 6-4, 11-9
1926	V. Richards – R.N. Williams	A. H. Chapin, Jr. – William T. Tilden	6-4, 6-8, 11-9, 6-3
1927	F.T. Hunter – W. T. Tilden	W. M. Johnston – R. N. Williams	10-8, 6-3, 6-3

1928	J.H. Doeg – G.M. Lott, Jr.	John B. Hawkes – G. L. Patterson	6-2, 6-1, 6-2
1929	J.H. Doeg – G.M. Lott, Jr.	Berkeley Bell – Lewis N. White	10-8, 1-6, 1-4, 6-1
1930	J.H. Doeg – G.M. Lott, Jr.	Wilmer L. Allison – John Van Ryn	8-6, 6-3, 3-6, 13-15, 6-4
1931	W.L. Allison – J. Van Ryn	Berkeley Bell – Gregory Mangin	6-4, 6-3, 6-2
1932	K. Gledhill – H.E. Vines	Wilmer L. Allison – John Van Ryn	6-4, 6-3, 6-2
1933	G.M. Lott, Jr.– L.R. Stoefen	Frank A. Parker – Francis X. Shields	11-13, 9-7, 9-7, 6-3
1934	G.M. Lott, Jr. – L.R. Stoefen	Wilmer L. Allison – John Van Ryn	6-4, 9-7, 3-6, 6-4
1935	W.L. Allison – J. Van Ryn	J. Donald Budge – C. Gene Mako	6-2, 6-3, 2-6, 3-6, 6-1
1936	J.D. Budge – C.G. Mako	Wilmer L. Allison – John Van Ryn	6-4, 6-2, 6-4
1937	B.G. von Cramm – H. Henkel	J. Donald Budge – C. Gene Mako	6-4, 7-5, 6-4
1938	J.D. Budge – C.G. Mako	John E. Bromwich – Adrian K. Quist	6-3, 6-2, 6-1
1939	J.E. Bromwich – A.K. Quist	J.A. Crawford – Harry C. Hopman	8-6, 6-1, 6-4
1940	J. Kramer – F.R. Schroeder, Jr.	Gardnar Mulloy – Henry J. Prussoff	6-4, 8-6, 9-7
1941	J. Kramer – F.R. Schroeder, Jr.	Wayne Gabin – Gardner Mulloy	9-7, 6-4, 6-2
1942	Lt. G. Mulloy – W.F. Talbert	F.R. Schroeder, Jr. – S.B. Wood, Jr.	9-7, 7-5, 6-1
1943	J. Kramer – F.A. Parker	David Freeman – William F. Talbert	6-2, 6-4, 6-4
1944	R. Falkenburg – Lt. W.D. McNeill	F. "Pancho" Segura – W. F. Talbert	7-5, 6-4, 3-6, 6-1
1945	Lt. G. Mulloy – W.F. Talbert	Robert Falkenburg – Jack Tuero	12-10, 8-10, 12-10, 6-2
1946	G. Mulloy – W. F. Talbert	F. Guernsey – W. Donald McNeill	3-6, 6-4, 2-6, 6-3, 20-18
1947	J. Kramer – F.R. Schroeder, Jr	William Sidwell – William F. Talbert	6-4, 7-5, 6-3
1948	G. Mulloy – W.F. Talbert	F.A. Parker – F. R. Schroeder, Jr.	1-6, 9-7, 6-3, 3-6, 9-7
1949	J.E. Bromwich – W. Sidwe	Frank Sedgman – G. Worthington	6-4, 6-0, 6-1
1950	J.E. Bromwich – F. Sedgman	Gardnar Mulloy – William F. Talbert	7-5, 8-6, 3-6, 6-1
1951	K. McGregor – F. Sedgman	Don Candy – Mervyn Rose	10-8, 6-4, 4-6, 7-5
1952	M. Rose – E.V. Seixas, Jr.	Kenneth McGregor – F. Sedgman	3-6, 10-8, 10-8, 6-8, 8-6
1953	Rex Hartwig – Frank Sedgman	Gardnar Mulloy – William F. Talbert	6-4, 4-6, 6-2, 6-4
1954	E.V. Seixas, Jr.– T. Trabert	Lewis Hoad – Kenneth Rosewall	3-6, 6-4, 8-6, 6-3
1955	Kosei Kamo – Atushi Miyagi	Gerald Moss – William Quillan	6-3, 6-3, 3-6, 1-6, 6-4
1956	L. Hoad – Kenneth Rosewall	H. Richardson – E. Victor Seixas, Jr.	6-2, 6-2, 3-6, 6-4
1957	A.J. Cooper – Neale Fraser	G. Mulloy – J. E. "Budge" Patty	4-6, 6-3, 9-7, 6-3
1958	A. Olmedo – H. Richardson	Sam Giammalva – Barry MacKay	3-6, 6-3, 6-4, 6-4
1959	R. Emerson – Neale Fraser	E. Buchholz, Jr. – A. "Alex" Olmedo	3-6, 6-3, 5-7, 6-4, 7-5
1960	R. Emerson – Neale Fraser	Rodney Laver – Robert Mark	9-7, 6-2, 6-4
1961	C. McKinley – D. Ralston	Rafael Osuna – Antonio Palafox	6-3, 6-4, 2-6, 13-11
1962	R. Osuna – Antonio Palafox	Charles McKinley – Dennis Ralston	6-4, 10-12, 1-6, 9-7, 6-3
1963	C. McKinley – D. Ralston	Rafael Osuna – Antonio Palafox	9-7, 4-6, 5-7, 6-3, 11-9
1964	C. McKinley – D. Ralston	Mike Sangster – Graham Stilwell	6-3, 6-2, 6-4
1965	Roy Emerson – Fred Stolle	F.Froehling, III – Charles Pasarell	6-4, 10-12, 7-5, 6-3
1966	Roy Emerson – Fred Stolle	Clark Graebner – Dennis Ralston	6-4, 6-4, 6-4
1967	J. Newcombe – Tony Roche	William Bowrey – Owen Davidson	6-8, 9-7, 6-3, 6-3
1968	Bob Lutz – Stan Smith	Arthur Ashe – Andres Gimeno	11-9, 6-1, 7-5

Open Era

1968	Bob Lutz – Stan Smith	Bob Hewitt - Ray Moore	6-4, 6-4, 9-7
1969	K. Rosewall – Fred Stolle	Charles Pasarell – Dennis Ralston	2-6, 7-5, 13-11, 6-3
1970	Pierre Barthes – Nikki Pilic	Roy Emerson – Rodney Laver	6-3, 7-6, 4-6, 7-6
1971	J. Newcombe – Roger Taylor	Stan Smith – Erik van Dillen	6-7, 6-3, 7-6, 4-6, (5-3)
1972	Cliff Drysdale – Roger Taylor	Owen Davidson – John Newcombe	6-4, 7-6, 6-3
1973	Owen Davidson – J. Newcombe	Rodney Laver – Kenneth Rosewall	7-5, 2-6, 7-5, 7-5
1974	Robert Lutz – Stan Smith	Patricio Cornejo – Jaime Fillol	6-3, 6-3
1975	Jimmy Connors – Ilie Nastase	Tom Okker – Marty Riessen	6-4, 7-6
1976	Tom Okker – Marty Riessen	Paul Kronk – Cliff Latcher	6-4, 6-0
1977	Bob Hewitt – F. McMillan	Brian Gottfried – Raul Ramirez	6-4, 6-0
1978	Robert Lutz – Stan Smith	M. Riessen – Sherwood Stewart	1-6, 7-5, 6-3
1979	Peter Fleming – John McEnroe	Robert Lutz – Stan Smith	6-2, 6-4
1980	Robert Lutz – Stan Smith	Peter Fleming – John McEnroe	7-6, 3-6, 6-1, 3-6, 6-3
1981	Peter Fleming – John McEnroe	Heinz Gunthardt – P. McNamara	Default
1982	K. Curren – Steve Denton	Victor Amaya – Hank Pfister	6-2, 6-7, 5-7, 6-2, 6-4
1983	Peter Fleming – John McEnroe	Fritz Buehning – Van Winitsky	6-3, 6-4, 6-2
1984	J. Fitzgerald – Tomas Smid	Stefan Edberg – Anders Jarryd	7-6, 6-3, 6-3
1985	Ken Flach – Robert Seguso	Henri Leconte – Yannick Noah	6-7, 7-6, 7-6, 6-0
1986	A. Gomez – S. Zivojinovic	Joakim Nystrom – Mats Wilander	4-6, 6-3, 6-3, 4-6, 6-3
1987	Stefan Edberg – A. Jarryd	Ken Flach – Robert Seguso	7-6, 6-2, 4-6, 5-7, 7-6
1988	Sergio Casal – E. Sanchez	Rick Leach – Jim Pugh	Walkover
1989	J. McEnroe – M. Woodforde	Ken Flach – Robert Seguso	6-4, 4-6, 6-3, 6-3
1990	P. Aldrich – Danie Visser	P. Annacone – D. Wheaton	6-2, 7-6, 6-2
1991	J. Fitzgerald – A. Jarryd	Scott Davis – David Pate	6-3, 3-6, 6-3, 6-3
1992	Jim Grabb – R. Reneberg	Kelly Jones – Rick Leach	3-6, 7-6, 6-3, 6-3
1993*	Ken Flach – Rick Leach	Martin Damm – Karel Novacek	6-7, 6-4, 6-2
1994	J. Eltingh – Paul Haarhuis	Todd Woodbridge – M. Woodforde	6-3, 8-6
1995	T. Woodbridge – M. Woodforde	Alex O'Brien – Sandon Stolle	6-3, 6-3
1996	T. Woodbridge – M. Woodforde	Jacco Eltingh – Paul Haarhuis	4-6, 7-6, 7-6
1997	Y. Kafelnikov – Daniel Vacek	Jonas Bjorkman – Nicklas Kulti	7-6, 6-3
1998	Sandon Stolle – Cyril Suk	Mark Knowles – Daniel Nestor	4-6, 7-6, 6-2
1999	S. Lareau – Alex O'Brien	Mahesh Bhupathi – Leander Paes	7-6, 6-4
2000	Lleyton Hewitt–Max Mirnyi	Ellis Ferreira – Rick Leach	6-4, 5-7, 7-6
2001	Wayne Black – Kevin Ullyett	Donald Johnson – Jared Palmer	7-6, 2-6, 6-3

* Year in which both amateur and professional events were held.

Women's Doubles

Year	Champions	Runners–up	Score
1889	M.L. Ballard – B.L. Townsend	Laura Knight – Marian Wright	6-0, 6-2
1890	E.C. Roosevelt – G.W. Roosevelt	M.L. Ballard – B.L. Townsend	6-1, 6-2
1891	M. Cahill – Mrs. W.F. Morgan	E.C. Roosevelt – G.W. Roosevelt	2-6, 8-6, 6-4
1892	Mabel Cahill – A. McKinlay	Mrs. A.H. Harris – Amy R. Williams	6-1, 6-3
1893	Hattie Butler – A.M. Terry	Augusta L. Schultz – Miss Stone	6-4, 6-3
1894	J.P. Atkinson – H. Hellwig	Amy R. Williams – A.C. Wistar	6-4, 8-6, 6-2
1895	J.P. Atkinson – H. Hellwig	Elisabeth H. Moore – A.R. Williams	6-2, 6-2, 12-10
1896	J.P. Atkinson – E.H. Moore	Amy R. Williams – A.C. Wistar	6-4, 7-5
1897	J.P. Atkinson – K. Atkinson	Mrs. F. Edwards – E.J. Rastall	6-2, 6-1, 6-1
1898	J.P. Atkinson – K. Atkinson	Carrie B. Neely – Marie Wimer	6-1, 2-6, 4-6, 6-1, 6-2
1899	J.W. Craven – M. McAteer	Maud Banks – Elizabeth J. Rastall	6-1, 6-1, 7-5
1900	H. Champlin – Edith Parker	Myrtle McAteer – Marie Wimer	9-7, 6-2, 6-2
1901	J.P. Atkinson – M. McAteer	Marion Jones – Elisabeth H. Moore	Default
1902	J.P. Atkinson – M. Jones	Maud Banks – Nona Closterman	6-2, 7-5
1903	E.H. Moore – C.B. Neely	Miriam Hall – Marion Jones	4-6, 6-1, 6-1
1904	M. Hall – May G. Sutton	Elisabeth Moore – Carrie B. Neely	3-6, 6-3, 6-3
1905	H. Homans – C.B. Neely	Virginia Maule – M.F. Oberteuffer	6-0, 6-1
1906	Mrs. L.S. Coe – Mrs. D.S. Platt	Clover Boldt – Helen Homans	6-4, 6-4
1907	Carrie B. Neely – Marie Wimer	Edna Wildey – Natalie Wildey	6-1, 2-6, 6-4
1908	Margaret Curtis – Evelyn Sears	Carrie B. Neely – Marion Steever	6-3, 5-7, 9-7
1909	H.V. Hotchkiss – E.E. Rotch	Dorothy Green – Lois Moyes	6-1, 6-1
1910	H.V. Hotchkiss – E.E. Rotch	Adelaide Browning – Edna Wildey	6-4, 6-4
1911	H.V. Hotchikss – E. Sears	Dorothy Green – Florence Sutton	6-4, 4-6, 6-2
1912	M.K. Browne – Dorothy Green	M. Barger–Wallach – Mrs. F. Schmitz	6-2, 5-7, 6-0
1913	M.K. Browne – Mrs. R.H. Williams	Dorothy Green – Edna Wildey	12-10, 2-6, 6-3
1914	M.K. Browne – Mrs. R.H. Williams	Louise H. Raymond – Edna Wildey	10-8, 6-2
1915	H.H. Wightman – E. Sears	Mrs. G. L. Chapman – H.H. McLean	10-8, 6-2
1916	M. Bjurstedt – E.a Sears	Louise H. Raymond – Edna Wildey	4-6, 6-2, 10-8
1917	Molla Bjurstedt – E. Sears	Mrs. Robert LeRoy – Phyllis Walsh	6-2, 6-4
1918	E.E. Goss – Marion Zinderstein	Molla Bjurstedt – Mrs. J. Rogge	7-5, 8-6
1919	E.E. Goss – Marion Zinderstein	E. Sears – H.H. Wightman	10-8, 9-7
1920	E.E. Goss – Marion Zinderstein	Helen Baker – Eleanor Tennant	6-3, 6-1
1921	M.K. Browne – Mrs. R.H. Williams	H. Gilleaudeau – Mrs. L.G. Morris	6-3, 6-2
1922	M.Z. Jessup – Helen Wills	Molla B. Mallory – Edith Sigourney	6-4, 7-9, 6-3
1923	P.H. Covell – K. "Kitty" McKane	E.E. Goss – H.H. Wightman	2-6, 6-2, 6-1
1924	H.H. Wightman – Helen Wills	Eleanor E. Goss – M. Z. Jessup	6-4, 6-3
1925	Mary K. Browne – Helen Wills	May S. Bundy – Elizabeth Ryan	6-4, 6-3
1926	E.E. Goss – Elizabeth Ryan	Mary K. Browne – C.H. Chapin	3-6, 6-4, 12-10
1927	K. "Kitty" Godfree – E. Harvey	Joan Fry – Betty Nuthall	6-1, 4-6, 6-4
1928	H.H. Wightman – Helen Wills	Edith Cross – Anna McCune Harper	6-2, 6-2
1929	P.S. Mitchell – P.H. Watson	P. Covel – Mrs. Shepherd–Barron	2-6, 6-3, 6-4
1930	Betty Nuthall – S.H. Palfrey	Edith Cross – Anna McCune Harper	3-6, 6-3, 7-5
1931	B. Nuthall – E.B. Whitingstall	Helen H. Jacobs – Dorothy Round	6-2, 6-4
1932	H.H. Jacobs – Sarah H. Palfrey	Edith Cross – Anna McCune Harper	3-6, 6-3, 7-5
1933	Freda James – Betty Nuthall	Helen Wills Moody – Elizabeth Ryan	Default
1934	H.H. Jacobs – S.H. Palfrey	Dorothy Andrus – C.A. Babcock	4-6, 6-3, 6-4
1935	H.H. Jacobs – S.Palfrey Fabyan	Dorothy Andrus – C.A. Babcock	6-4, 6-2
1936	C.A. Babcock – M.G. Van Ryn	H.H. Jacobs – S. Palfrey Fabyan	9-7, 2-6, 6-4
1937	A. Marble – S. Palfrey Fabyan	C.A. Babcock – M.G. Van Ryn	7-5, 6-4
1938	A. Marble – S. Palfrey Fabyan	J. Jedrzejowska – Rene Mathieu	6-8, 6-4, 6-3
1939	A. Marble – S. Palfrey Fabyan	F. Hammersley – K. Stammers	7-5, 8-6
1940	A. Marble – S. Palfrey Fabyan	Dorothy Bundy – M.G. Van Ryn	6-4, 6-3
1941	M.E. Osborne – S.P. Fabyan	Pauline Betz – Dorothy Bundy	3-6, 6-1, 6-4
1942	A.L. Brough – M.E. Osborne	Pauline Betz – Doris Hart	2-6, 7-5, 6-0
1943	A.L. Brough – M.E. Osborne	Mary A. Prentiss – Patricia C. Todd	6-1, 6-3
1944	A.L. Brough – M.E. Osborne	Pauline Betz – Doris Hart	4-6, 6-4, 6-3
1945	A.L. Brough – M.E. Osborne	Pauline Betz – Doris Hart	6-3, 6-3
1946	A.L. Brough – M.E. Osborne	M.A Prentiss – Patricia C. Todd	6-1, 6-3
1947	A.L. Brough – M.E. Osborne	Doris Hart – Patricia C. Todd	5-7, 6-3, 7-5
1948	A.L. Brough – M.E. Osborne	Doris Hart – Patricia C. Todd	6-4, 8-10, 6-1
1949	A.L. Brough – M.E. Osborne	Doris Hart – Shirley Fry	6-4, 10-8
1950	A.L. Brough – M.E. Osborne	Doris Hart – Shirley Fry	6-2, 6-3
1951	Shirley Fry – Doris Hart	Nancy Chaffee– Patricia C. Todd	6-4, 6-2
1952	Shirley Fry – Doris Hart	A. Louise Brough – M. Connolly	10-8, 6-4
1953	Shirley Fry – Doris Hart	A.L. Brough – M. Osborne duPont	6-2, 7-9, 9-7
1954	Shirley Fry – Doris Hart	A.L. Brough – M. Osborne duPont	6-4, 6-4
1955	A.L. Brough – M.O. duPont	Shirley Fry – Doris Hart	6-3, 1-6, 6-3
1956	A.L. Brough – M.O. duPont	Shirley Fry – Betty R. Pratt	6-3, 6-0
1957	A.L. Brough – M.O. duPont	Althea Gibson –Darlene R. Hard	6-2, 7-5
1958	J.M. Arth – Darlene R. Hard	Maria Bueno – Althea Gibson	2-6, 6-3, 6-4
1959	J.M. Arth – Darlene R. Hard	Althea Gibson – Sally Moore	6-2, 6-3
1960	Maria Bueno – D.R. Hard	Deidre Catt – Ann Haydon	6-1, 6-1
1961	D.R. Hard – Lesley Turner	Edda Buding – Yola Ramirez	6-4, 5-7, 6-0
1962	Maria Bueno – D.R. Hard	Billie Jean Moffitt – K.H. Susman	4-6, 6-3, 6-2
1963	R. Ebbern – Margaret Smith	Maria Bueno – Darlene R. Hard	4-6, 10-8, 6-3

1964	B. J. Moffitt – K.H. Susman	Margaret Smith – Lesley Turner	3-6, 6-2, 6-4
1965	C.C. Graebner – N. Richey	Billie Jean Moffitt – K.H. Susman	6-4, 6-4
1966	Maria Bueno – Nancy Richey	Rosemary Casals – B.J. Moffitt	6-3, 6-4
1967	R. Casals – Billie Jean King	Mary Ann Eisel – Donna Floyd Fales	4-6, 6-3, 6-4
Open Era			
1968	M. Bueno – M. Smith Court	Rosemary Casals – Billie Jean King	4-6, 9-7, 8-6
1969	F. Durr – Darlene R. Hard	Margaret Smith Court – V. Wade	0-6, 6-4, 6-4
1970	M.S. Court – J. Tegart Dalton	Rosemary Casals – Virginia Wade	6-3, 6-4
1971	R. Casals – J. Tegart Dalton	Gail Chanfreau – Francoise Durr	6-3, 6-3
1972	Francoise Durr – Betty Stove	Margaret Smith Court – V. Wade	6-3, 1-6, 6-3
1973	M. Smith Court – V. Wade	Rosemary Casals – Billie Jean King	3-6, 6-3, 7-5
1974	R. Casals – Billie Jean King	Francoise Durr – Betty Stove	7-6, 6-7, 6-4
1975	M. Smith Court – V. Wade	Rosemary Casals – Billie Jean King	7-5, 2-6, 7-5
1976	Delina Boshoff – Ilana Kloss	Olga Morozova – Virginia Wade	6-1, 6-4
1977	M. Navratilova – Betty Stove	Renee Richards – Bettyann Stuart	6-1, 7-6
1978	B.J. King – Martina Navratilova	Kerry Melville Reid – Wendy Turnbull	7-6, 6-4
1979	Betty Stove – Wendy Turnbull	Billie Jean King – M. Navratilova	7-5, 6-3
1980	B.J. King – Martina Navratilova	Pam Shriver – Betty Stove	7-6, 7-5
1981	Kathy Jordan – Anne Smith	Rosemary Casals – Wendy Turnbull	6-3, 6-3
1982	R. Casals – Wendy Turnbull	Barbara Potter – Sharon Walsh	6-4, 6-4
1983	M. Navratilova – Pam Shriver	Rosalyn Fairbank – Candy Reynolds	6-7, 6-1, 6-3
1984	M. Navratilova – Pam Shriver	Anne Hobbs – Wendy Turnbull	6-2, 6-4
1985	C. Kohde–Kilsch – H. Sukova	Martina Navratilova – Pam Shriver	6-7, 6-2, 6-3
1986	M. Navratilova – Pam Shriver	Hana Mandlikova – Wendy Turnbull	6-4, 3-6, 6-3
1987	M. Navratilova – Pam Shriver	Kathy Jordan – Elizabeth Smylie	5-7, 6-4, 6-2
1988	Gigi Fernandez – Robin White	Patty Fendick – Jill Hetherington	6-4, 6-1
1989	H. Mandlikova – M. Navratilova	Mary Joe Fernandez – Pam Shriver	5-7, 6-4, 6-4
1990	G. Fernandez – M. Navratilova	Jana Novotna – Helena Sukova	6-2, 6-4
1991	Pam Shriver – Natalia Zvereva	Jana Novotna – Larisa Savchenko	6-4, 4-6, 7-6
1992	G. Fernandez – N. Zvereva	Jana Novotna – Larisa Savchenko	7-6, 6-1
1993	A. Sanchez-Vicario – H. Sukova	A. Coetzer – Ines Gorrochategui	6-4, 6-2
1994	J. Novotna – A. Sanchez-Vicario	Katerina Maleeva – Robin White	6-3, 6-3
1995	G. Fernandez – N. Zvereva	B. Schultz–McCarthy – R. Stubbs	7-5, 6-3
1996	G. Fernandez – N. Zvereva	J. Novotna – A. Sanchez-Vicario	1-6, 6-1, 6-4
1997	L. Davenport – Jana Novotna	Gigi Fernandez – Natasha Zvereva	6-3, 6-4
1998	M. Hingis – Jana Novotna	Lindsay Davenport – N. Zvereva	6-3, 6-3
1999	S. Williams – Venus Williams	Chanda Rubin – Sandrine Testud	4-6, 6-1, 6-4
2000	J. Halard–Decugis – A. Sugiyama	Cara Black – Elena Likhovtseva	6-0, 1-6, 6-1
2001	L. Raymond – Rennae Stubbs	K. Po-Messerli – Nathalie Tauziat	6-2, 5-7, 7-5

Mixed Doubles

Year	Champions	Runners-up	Score
1892	Mabel Cahill – C. Hobart	Elisabeth Moore – R.V. Beach	6-1, 6-3
1893	Ellen C. Roosevelt – C. Hobart	Ethel Bankston – R.N. Willson, Jr.	6-1, 4-6, 10-6, 6-1
1894	J.P. Atkinson – E.P. Fischer	Mrs. McFadden – G. Remak, Jr.	6-3, 6-2, 6-1
1895	J.P. Atkinson – E.P. Fischer	Amy R. Williams – Mantle Fielding	4-6, 8-6, 6-2
1896	J.P. Atkinson – E.P. Fischer	Amy R. Williams – Mantle Fielding	6-2, 6-3, 6-3
1897	L. Henson – D.L. Magruder	Maud Banks – R.A. Griffin	6-4, 6-3, 7-5
1898	C.B. Neely – Edwin P. Fischer	Helen Chapman – J. A. Hill	6-2, 6-4, 8-6
1899	E.J. Rastall – A.L. Hoskins	Jane W. Craven – J.P. Gardner	6-4, 6-0, def.
1900	M. Hunnewell – A. Codman	Isabelle Shaw – George Atkinson	11-9, 6-3, 6-1
1901	M. Jones – Raymond D. Little	Myrtle McAteer – Dr. Clyde Stevens	6-4, 6-4, 7-5
1902	E. Moore – Wylie C. Grant	Elizabeth J. Rastall – A.L. Hoskins	6-2, 6-1
1903	Helen Chapman – H.F. Allen	Carrie B. Neely – W.H. Rowland	6-4, 7-5
1904	El. Moore – Wylie C. Grant	May G. Sutton – F.B. Dallas	6-2, 6-1
1905	A. Schultz Hobart – C. Hobart	Elisabeth Moore – E.B. Dewhurst	6-2, 6-4
1906	Sarah Coffin – E.B. Dewhurst	Margaret Johnson – J.B. Johnson	6-3, 7-5
1907	May Sayres – W.F. Johnson	Natalie Wildey – H. Morris Tilden	6-1, 7-5
1908	Edith E. Rotch – N.W. Niles	L. Hammond – Raymond D. Little	6-4, 4-6, 6-4
1909	H.V. Hotchkiss – W.F. Johnson	L. Hammond – Raymond D. Little	6-2, 6-0
1910	H.V. Hotchkiss – J. Carpenter, Jr.	Edna Wildey – H. Morris Tilden	6-2, 6-2
1911	H.V. Hotchkiss – W.F. Johnson	Edna Wildey – H. Morris Tilden	6-4, 6-4
1912	M.K. Browne – R.N. Williams	Eleanora Sears – W.J. Clothier	6-4, 2-6, 11-9
1913	M.K. Browne – W.T. Tilden	Dorothy Green – C.S. Rogers	7-5, 7-5
1914	M.K. Browne – W.T. Tilden	Margaretta Myers – J.R. Rowland	6-1, 6-4
1915	H.H. Wightman – H.C. Johnson	Molla Bjurstedt – Irving C. Wright	6-0, 6-1
1916	E. Sears – Willis F. Davis	Florence A. Ballin – William T. Tilden	6-4, 7-5
1917	M. Bjurstedt – I.C. Wright	Florence A. Ballin – William T. Tilden	10-12, 6-1, 6-3
1918	H.H. Wightman – I.C. Wright	Molla Bjurstedt – F.B. Alexander	6-2, 6-3
1919	M. Zinderstein – V. Richards	Florence A. Ballin – William T. Tilden	2-6, 11-9, 6-2
1920	H.H. Wightman – W.F. Johnson	Molla B. Mallory – Craig Biddle	6-4, 6-3
1921	M.K. Browne – W.M. Johnston	Molla B. Mallory – William T. Tilden	3-6, 6-4, 6-3
1922	M.K. Browne – William T. Tilden	Helen Wills – Howard Kinsey	6-4, 6-3
1923	M.B. Mallory – William T. Tilden	K. "Kitty" McKane – John B. Hawkes	6-3, 2-6, 10-8
1924	Helen Wills – Vincent Richards	Molla B. Mallory – William T. Tilden	6-8, 7-5, 6-0
1925	K. "Kitty" McKane – J.B. Hawkes	Er. Harvey – Vincent Richards	6-2, 6-4
1926	Elizabeth Ryan – Jean Borotra	H.H. Wightman – Rene LaCoste	6-4, 7-5
1927	Eileen Bennett – Henri Cochet	H.H. Wightman – Rene LaCoste	6-2, 6-0, 6-3
1928	Helen Wills – John B. Hawkes	Edith Cross – Edgar F. Moon	6-1, 6-3
1929	Betty Nuthall – G.M. Lott, Jr.	Phyllis Covell – Henry W. Austin	6-3, 6-3
1930	Edith Cross – Wilmer L. Allison	Marjorie Morrill – Francis X. Shields	6-4, 6-4
1931	Betty Nuthall – G.M. Lott, Jr.	Anna McCune Harper – W.L. Allison	6-3, 6-3
1932	Sarah H. Palfrey – Fred Perry	Helen H. Jacobs – H.E. Vines	6-3, 7-5
1933	E. Ryan – H. Ellsworth Vines	Sarah H. Palfrey – G.M. Lott, Jr.	11-9, 6-1
1934	H.H. Jacobs – G.M. Lott, Jr.	Elizabeth Ryan – Lester R. Stoefen	4-6, 13-11, 6-2
1935	S.P. Fabyan – Enrique Maier	Kay Stammers – Roderick Menzel	6-4, 4-6, 6-3
1936	Alice Marble – C. Gene Mako	S.P. Fabyan – J. Donald Budge	6-3, 6-2
1937	S.P. Fabyan – J. Donald Budge	Sylvia Henrotin – Yvon Petra	6-2, 8-10, 6-0
1938	Alice Marble – J. Donald Budge	Thelma Coyne – John E. Bromwich	6-1, 6-2
1939	Alice Marble – H.C. Hopman	S.P. Fabyan – E. Cooke	9-7 6-1
1940	Alice Marble – Robert L. Riggs	D. Bundy – Jack Kramer	9-7 6-1
1941	S.Palfrey Cooke – Jack Kramer	P. Betz – Robert L. Riggs	4-6, 6-4, 6-4
1942	A.L. Brough – F.R. Schroeder, Jr.	P.C. Todd – A. Russell	3-6, 6-1, 6-4
1943	M.E. Osborne – W.F. Talbert	P. Betz – Pancho Segura	10-6, 6-4
1944	M.E. Osborne – W.F. Talbert	D. Bundy – Lt. W.D. McNeill	6-2, 6-3
1945	M.E. Osborne – W.F. Talbert	D. Hart – R. Falkenberg	6-4, 6-4
1946	M.E. Osborne – W.F. Talbert	A.Louisee Brough – R. Kimbrell	6-3, 6-4
1947	A.L. Brough – J.E. Bromwich	G. Moran – Pancho Segura	6-3, 6-1
1948	A.L. Brough – T.P. Brown, Jr.	M.O. duPont – William F. Talbert	6-4, 6-4
1949	A.L. Brough – Eric Sturgess	M.O. duPont – William F. Talbert	4-6, 6-3, 7-5
1950	M.O. duPont – K. McGregor	Doris Hart – Frank Sedgman	6-4, 3-6, 6-3
1951	Doris Hart – Frank Sedgman	Shirley Fry – Mervyn Rose	6-3, 6-2
1952	Doris Hart – Frank Sedgman	Thelma C. Long,– Lewis Hoad	6-3, 7-5
1953	Doris Hart – E.V. Seixas, Jr.	Julia Ann Sampson – Rex Hartwig	6-2, 4-6, 6-4
1954	D. Hart – E. Victor Seixas, Jr.	M.O. duPont – Kenneth Rosewall	4-6, 6-1, 6-1
1955	D. Hart – E. Victor Seixas, Jr.	Shirley Fry – Lewis Hoad	9-7, 6-1
1956	M.O. duPont – K. Rosewall	Darlene R. Hard – Lewis Hoad	9-7, 6-1
1957	Althea Gibson – Kurt Nelson	Darlene R. Hard – Bob Howe	6-3, 9-7
1958	M.O. duPont – Neale Fraser	Maria Bueno – A. "Alex" Olmedo	6-3, 3-6, 9-7
1959	M.O. duPont – Neale Fraser	Janet Hopps – Robert Mark	7-5, 13-15, 6-2
1960	M.O. duPont – Neale Fraser	Maria Bueno – Antonio Palafox	6-3, 6-2
1961	M. Smith – Robert Mark	Darlene R. Hard – Dennis Ralston	def.
1962	M. Smith – Fred Stolle	Lesley Turner – Frank Froehling, III	7-5, 6-2
1963	M. Smith – Ken Fletcher	Judy Tegart – Ed Rubinoff	3-6, 8-6, 6-2
1964	M. Smith – John Newcombe	Judy Tegart – Ed Rubinoff	10-6, 4-6, 6-3
1965	Margaret Smith – Fred Stolle	Judy Tegart – Frank Froehling III	6-2, 6-2
1966	D. Floyd Fales – Owen Davidson	Carol H. Aucamp – Ed Rubinoff	6-1, 6-3
1967	B.J. King – Owen Davidson	Rosemary Casals – Stan Smith	6-3, 6-2
Open Era			
1968	M.A. Eisel – Peter Curtis	Tory Fretz – Gerry Perry	6-4, 7-5
1969	M. Smith Court – M. Riessen	Francoise Durr – Dennis Ralston	7-5, 6-3
1970	M. Smith Court – M. Riessen	J. Tegart Dalton – Frew McMillan	6-4, 6-4
1971	Billie Jean King – O. Davidson	Betty Stove – Rob Maud	6-3, 7-5
1972	M. Smith Court – M. Riessen	Rosemary Casals – Ilie Nastase	6-3, 7-5
1973	Billie Jean King – O. Davidson	M. Smith Court – Marty Riessen	6-3, 3-6, 7-6
1974	P. Teeguarden – Geoff Masters	Chris Evert – Jimmy Connors	6-1, 7-6
1975	R. Casals – Richard Stockton	Billie Jean King – Fred Stolle	6-3, 7-6
1976	Billie Jean King – Phil Dent	Betty Stove – Frew McMillan	3-6, 6-2, 7-5
1977	Betty Stove – Frew McMillan	Billie Jean King – Vitas Gerulaitis	6-2, 3-6, 6-3
1978	Betty Stove – Frew McMillan	Billie Jean King – Ray Ruffels	6-3, 7-6
1979	Greer Stevens – Bob Hewitt	Betty Stove – Frew McMillan	6-3, 7-5
1980	Wendy Turnbull – M. Riessen	Betty Stove – Frew McMillan	7-5, 6-2
1981	Anne Smith – Kevin Curren	JoAnne Russell – Steve Denton	6-4, 7-6
1982	Anne Smith – Kevin Curren	Barbara Potter – Ferdi Taygan	6-7, 7-6, 7-6
1983	E. Sayers – John Fitzgerald	Barbara Potter – Ferdi Taygan	3-6, 6-3, 6-4
1984	M. Maleeva – Tom Gullikson	Elizabeth Sayers – John Fitzgerald	2-6, 7-5, 6-4
1985	M. Navratilova – H. Gunthardt	Elizabeth Smylie – John Fitzgerald	6-3, 6-4
1986	Raffaella Reggi – Sergio Casal	Martina Navratilova – Peter Fleming	6-4, 6-4
1987	M. Navratilova – Emilio Sanchez	Betsy Nagelsen – Paul Annacone	6-4, 6-7, 7-6
1988	Jana Novotna – Jim Pugh	Elizabeth Smylie – Patrick McEnroe	7-5, 6-3
1989	Robin White – Shelby Cannon	Meredith McGrath – Rick Leach	3-6, 6-2, 7-5
1990	E. Smylie – Todd Woodbridge	Natalia Zvereva – Jim Pugh	6-4, 6-2
1991	Manon Bollegraf – Tom Nijssen	A. Sanchez-Vicario – Emilio Sanchez	6-2, 7-6
1992	Nicole Provis – M. Woodforde	Helena Sukova – Tom Nijssen	4-6, 6-3, 6-3
1993	Helena Sukova – T. Woodbridge	M. Navratilova – Mark Woodforde	6-3, 7-6
1994	E. Reinach – Patrick Galbraith	Jana Novotna – Todd Woodbridge	6-2, 6-4
1995	M. McGrath – Matt Lucena	Gigi Fernandez – Cyril Suk	6-4, 6-4
1996	Lisa Raymond – P. Galbraith	Manon Bollegraf – Rick Leach	7-6, 7-6
1997	Manon Bollegraf – Rick Leach	Mercedes Paz – Pablo Albano	3-6, 7-5, 7-6
1998	Serena Williams – Max Mirnyi	Lisa Raymond – Patrick Galbraith	6-2, 6-2
1999	Ai Sugiyama – M. Bhupathi	Kimberly Po – Donald Johnson	6-4, 6-4
2000	A. Sanchez-Vicario – J. Palmer	Anna Kournikova – Max Mirnyi	6-4, 6-3
2001	R. Stubbs – T. Woodbridge	Lisa Raymond – Leander Paes	6-4, 5-7, 7-6

Contributors

Peter Bodo, a columnist for *The New York Times* and a senior writer for *Tennis,* has been covering professional tennis for more than two decades. His books include *The Courts of Babylon* and *Tennis for Dummies.*

Mary Carillo, a commentator for CBS Sports and TNT, competed on the women's professional tennis tour for four years. She is the author of *Tennis My Way* and *Tennis Kinetics.*

Bud Collins, a commentator for NBC Sports and a columnist for the *Boston Globe* and *Sports Business Journal,* is the author of a half dozen books, including *Bud Collins' Tennis Encyclopedia.* He has been inducted into the International Tennis Hall of Fame and the National Sportswriters and Sports Broadcasters Hall of Fame.

Joel Drucker is a journalist who has written about tennis for dozens of broadcast and print media, including CBS, HBO, TNT, *Tennis,* and *USTA Magazine.* He served as technical editor of *Tennis for Dummies.*

John Feinstein, a commentator for National Public Radio and ESPN, is the author of such bestsellers as *The Last Amateurs*, *The Majors*, and *A Good Walk Spoiled.* His latest book, *The Punch*, is being published this fall.

Steve Flink, a senior correspondent for *Tennis Week* and journalist and commentator on radio and television, is the author of *The Greatest Tennis Matches of the Twentieth Century.*

Photography Credits